Also by the Author

Punch Drunk

The Erin O'Reilly Mysteries
Book Fifteen

Steven Henry

Clickworks Press • Baltimore, MD

First publication: Clickworks Press, 2022
Release: CWP-EOR15.INT-P.ALL-1.0

Sign up for updates, deals, and exclusive sneak peeks at clickworkspress.com/join.

Ebook ISBN: 1-943383-88-7
Paperback ISBN: 978-1-943383-89-4
Hardcover ISBN: 1-943383-90-0

For Ben Faroe, my publisher, representative, and friend,
without whom this journey would have been
a shorter one with a worse ending.

Punch Drunk

Punch

A large number of drinks, served either hot or cold; usually a combination of hard liquor, wine, or beer mixed with a nonalcoholic beverage. Popular at parties, it is normally served in a punch bowl and ladled into cups.

Punch Drunk

The condition of being dazed or stupefied as a result of being struck in the head.

Chapter 1

The buzz of her phone cut through Erin O'Reilly's sleep, invading her dreams like a mosquito crawling into her ear. She shook her head, rolled over, and fumbled for the phone. It kept insistently buzzing, vibrating its way toward the edge of the nightstand. She caught it just before it passed the tipping point, lifted it, and looked at the caller ID.

The Smartphone's screen cast a green glow on her face. The name on it was SHELLEY. That meant her sister-in-law's cell phone. And the clock at the top of the screen read 1:52.

The bottom dropped out of Erin's stomach and she was suddenly awake and scared. She'd thought the call would be from work, a Patrol unit stumbling across a body. But murder was an everyday part of the Job and nothing to get excited about. A call from a family member at two in the morning meant *trouble.*

She glanced to one side and saw an unoccupied pillow, the bed half-made, its fine silk sheets smooth and empty. Carlyle, her boyfriend, must not have come up yet. That wasn't unusual. Pub owners and gangsters lived by night, and Carlyle was both. He was probably hanging out with other Irish Mob associates at the bar downstairs.

At the foot of the bed, a pair of anxious eyes reflected the phone's light in flashes of greenish white. Rolf had also been roused by the phone. Now the German Shepherd K-9 was watching her, head tilted to one side, wondering what was happening.

Erin took a breath and thumbed the phone. "Hello?" she said.

Her imagination filled the silence on the line with a whole parade of horrors, waking nightmares with names like cancer, car crash, and heart attack. Names danced through her head. Michelle wouldn't be calling about Erin's mom or dad, would she? Shelley's husband Sean Junior, maybe? Or one of the kids? Dear God, Erin thought, not Anna or Patrick. Please, not them.

"Erin?" The voice was distorted. Maybe they had a bad connection. It sounded a little like Michelle.

"Shelley? Is that you?"

"Erin, I... I didn't mean to wake you up. I'm sorry."

"I'm up now, Shelley," Erin said, throwing the sheets down to her waist and sitting up. "What's the matter? Is everyone okay? Junior? The kids?"

"They're... fine," Michelle said. Erin heard a really strange sound, a rapid-fire clicking that she couldn't identify.

"Are you okay, Shelley? Talk to me. Are you hurt?"

"Can... can I see you? Will you be up for a little while?"

"I'm hardly going to go back to sleep now," Erin said, fatigue and worry making her voice sharper than she meant it to be. "Do you need me to come over?"

"No, I... oh, I'd better not come to your place. Can we meet at that coffee shop? The one just down the block from you?"

"Java Passion?"

"That's the one."

"Sure." Erin flicked on the bedside lamp. She pivoted and

stood up, walking to the closet to get a pair of pants. "Are you driving from your house?" Michelle lived in a Midtown brownstone, about twenty minutes away.

Michelle hesitated. "No," she said, her voice still sounding odd. "I'm close by. I can be there in five minutes."

"Give me ten," Erin said. "I have to get dressed. Shelley, are you okay? Look, if you're in some sort of trouble, I can help, but I need to know. If it's an emergency, you'd better call 911. Patrol units can get to you faster than I can. Are you in danger?"

"I don't..." Michelle started to say. Then she cut herself off and that strange clicking sound came again. "I'll explain when I see you." Then, with a beep, the call disconnected.

Erin stared at her phone. That call had been as unlike Michelle as any conversation she could remember. Her sister-in-law was bright, vivacious, warm, and cheerful. And she never just hung up on someone.

Erin dressed as quickly as she could, just a T-shirt and jeans over her underwear. It was June, the New York weather was mild, and this was a late-night meeting. She didn't have to bother with makeup or fancy hairstyles. She pulled her hair back into a plain ponytail. She slipped her feet into her everyday shoes, a good, sensible pair which cheated her height up to five-foot-eight. Then she opened the nightstand drawer and took out her shield and her guns; her service sidearm, the Glock nine-millimeter, went on her belt and her backup piece, the snub-nosed .38 revolver, clipped to her right ankle. Both guns had saved her life before. It wasn't that she was expecting that sort of trouble. The weapons were just part of her wardrobe. She'd no more go out without them than run down the street barefoot.

She clipped the gold NYPD shield to her belt beside her holster. As she closed the drawer, she saw Rolf again. The Shepherd was standing now, tail waving uncertainly. He loved Erin's morning ritual of dressing and arming, because it meant they were going to work. Work was the best thing in the world. But he could tell she was worried, and that confused him.

"*Komm*," she said, speaking the command in the language he'd been trained in by his Bavarian breeders. That one word got him moving. He pranced beside her, wagging more enthusiastically. He was ready. Maybe there'd be bad guys to chase. If he was really lucky, maybe he'd get to bite one and be told what a good, brave boy he was. And then he'd get his rubber Kong ball and life would be great.

Erin opened the door at the bottom of the apartment's stairs. A flood of voices washed over her, the loud, happy chatter of a late-night public house. She stepped into the back of the Barley Corner's main room. The place was packed. She thanked God, and good building contractors, for the soundproofing that insulated the upstairs apartment. She couldn't see Carlyle in the crowd, but she knew he'd be at the bar in his place of honor.

She threaded her way over, keeping Rolf close on his leash. She found the silver-haired Irishman engaged in conversation with a pair of rough-looking guys. She recognized one of them, so knew they were with the Teamsters Union.

"Hey, Wayne," she said to one of the truckers by way of greeting. "How's the Beast?"

Wayne's face lit up. A big, burly guy, he'd given Erin a ride back to New York as a favor once, a favor she'd repaid by keeping him out of jail. The Beast was his truck, his pride and joy.

"She's running like a champ," he said. "How're you, miss? Share a drink with us?"

Carlyle had gotten to his feet when he saw her, only a hint of hitch in the motion. He'd almost completely recovered from the bullet that had nearly killed him earlier that spring, but some of his muscles hadn't quite gotten their old tone back. He gave her a quick, sharp glance. He didn't miss much.

"What brings you down, darling?" he asked in his Belfast brogue.

"I need to step out for a little. Got some family business."

"All well?" he asked, his face growing more concerned. Like Erin, he knew that family news in the wee hours was rarely good.

"I think so. I'll just be down the street. I should be back in an hour, at the most." She gave him a quick kiss on the cheek, marveling on the inside. Just a couple of months ago, she wouldn't have dared show any affection for him in public. But now their relationship was known both to the NYPD and the underworld. It wasn't that they weren't deceiving anyone. It was more that the deception had shifted onto new ground.

"I think I'll wait up for you," he said with a smile. "The night's young yet."

"The drink will have to wait," she said to Wayne. "Business first."

"Always," he agreed pleasantly. "Catch you later, Miss O'Reilly."

As she and Rolf walked toward the front door, she caught Wayne's words to Carlyle.

"—a lucky guy," he was saying. "I know guys would kill for a girl like that."

She smiled. What woman didn't want to hear herself described that way? She nodded a greeting to Caitlin, one of the Corner's waitresses, on the way out. The perky redhead grinned and waved to her. At least some folks seemed to be having a good night.

* * *

The night air, pleasantly cool, finished clearing Erin's head. The coffee shop was just a couple of storefronts down from the

Barley Corner. She let Rolf sniff some things and cock a leg at an alley entrance. As long as they were up, they might as well get a little walk out of it.

Java Passion was open twenty-four hours a day, but at this ungodly hour, not too many patrons were there. Most of them appeared to be taking advantage of the coffee shop's Wi-Fi and were concentrating on their laptops. But one customer, a tall, striking, dark-haired woman, was standing at the front window, a cup of coffee in one hand, the other wrapped around her own elbow. The cup was shaking. As Erin walked up to her, a little coffee sloshed over the brim.

"Hey, Shelley," Erin said.

Michelle O'Reilly nodded jerkily. "Thanks for coming," she said. Her eyes were puffy and bloodshot, like she'd been crying.

Erin put a hand on Michelle's shoulder and almost jerked her hand back on contact. Her sister-in-law was trembling like a live electric wire. "Let's sit down," she said.

"Do you want to get something?" Michelle asked, cocking her head toward the front counter.

"No, thanks." In truth, Erin could've used a cup of something hot, or better yet a shot of whiskey, to steady her nerves. But she had an odd feeling like Michelle might vanish if she turned her back, maybe bolt and run. She heard that clicking sound once more, and finally recognized what it was. Michelle's jaw was clenched so tight, her teeth were chattering.

They sat at a table along the side wall. No one paid them any attention. Rolf, his ambitions for an early workday thwarted, settled at Erin's feet with a sigh and closed his eyes. Michelle clutched her coffee cup in both hands, drawing comfort from the heat. She stared into the cup.

Erin was an experienced cop. She'd done dozens of interrogations. If Michelle had been a suspect in her interrogation room, Erin would've recognized all the "guilty" signs. Shifty body language, lack of eye contact, nervous tension.

She reached out and gently touched the back of Michelle's hand. "Hey, sis," she said. "What's wrong?"

"I think I screwed up," Michelle said. "Big time."

Erin's stomach made a flip-flop. "What do you mean?"

"Erin, I'm an only child," Michelle said. "You know that. One of the things... one of the things about... Sean is his big, tight family. You... you've always made me feel like I belong. With you."

"Of course," Erin said. "It doesn't matter if you're born one of us or if you marry in. You're an O'Reilly."

"I think of you like my sister," Michelle said.

"That's because you are," Erin said. That earned her a weak, watery smile and the briefest bit of eye contact.

"Thanks. So I'm asking... I'm begging you. Don't tell Sean what I'm about to tell you."

A cold feeling crept through Erin's midsection. "Shelley, he's your husband, and he's my brother."

"Promise!" Michelle snapped with sudden, brittle energy.

"Okay, okay," Erin said. "I promise." But even as she said it, she wondered what she was getting herself into.

"He's working tonight," Michelle said. That wasn't unusual. Sean O'Reilly Junior was a trauma surgeon at Bellevue Hospital and often worked the late shift in the emergency room.

"Okay," Erin said again.

"I... I wasn't at home," Michelle said softly.

"Where are the kids?" Erin asked. She was surprised when Michelle flinched at the question.

"Home. In bed. Asleep."

"You got a sitter, right?"

"Of course I did! Sam Perkins, from up the street. She's home from college for the summer and she's used to late hours."

"Shelley? Where were you?"

"I went to a dance club," Michelle said.

"Which one?"

"What does it matter? Stop being a cop for one second, Erin!"

"Okay, sorry. Old habits. Just tell me what you want to."

"I went out dancing. And I... I wasn't alone."

Erin swallowed. "I'm guessing you're not talking about one of your girlfriends."

Michelle shook her head.

"A guy you know?" Erin asked.

A nod.

"What happened?"

"We danced and had a few drinks," Michelle said. "Then he... he asked if I wanted to go back to his place. With him."

"Shelley," Erin said softly. She didn't even know what she was trying to say. Surprise, anger at the betrayal of her brother, concern, all of it jumbled together in her head.

"We got there and he... we went up to his apartment. And he made us cocktails, and we sat down on his couch, and we were talking and then... then we weren't..." Michelle's eyes filled with tears. One of them started rolling down her cheek. She didn't seem to notice it.

A part of Erin wanted to reach out and touch Michelle, to give her some comfort, but she sat back and watched. Now she was feeling a kind of clinical detachment, and that disturbed her. She liked Michelle. Hell, she *loved* her. But this was her brother's wife, talking about having an affair. What was she supposed to do with that information? And she'd been sworn to secrecy. Under the detachment, she felt a rising anger. How dare Shelley make her promise to keep something like this a secret?

"He was... he was really... it was..." Michelle faltered and didn't seem to know what to say.

"I hope it was worth it," Erin said grimly.

"No. It wasn't. I mean, it was good, at first. But I got scared. I haven't... I mean, not with any other guy. Not since Sean. So I panicked. I pushed him away. We didn't... you know. Not all the way. And I grabbed my... my shirt and things. And I got out of there."

Erin sagged back in her chair. "So you didn't go to bed with him?"

Michelle shook her head. "But I was going to," she said miserably. "I thought I wanted to. I *did* want to. But there, on his couch, I heard Anna's voice, like she was talking to me. And I thought, how am I going to explain this to her? Isn't that weird? I should've been thinking about Sean. Oh God, Erin, I'm the worst wife in the world."

"Sounds to me like you had a near miss," Erin said. "Think of this as a wake-up call. Whatever's gone wrong between the two of you, get to work on it. Make it right. I love you, Shelley, and I don't want to see your marriage blow up over some stupid bullshit you and Junior weren't willing to fix. That goes for him, too."

"You're not going to tell him," Michelle said. "Are you? You promised."

"I'm not going to tell him," Erin said. "Because you are."

"Are you crazy?" Michelle was horrified. "He'd kill me! And it'd wreck him. It'd break his heart."

Erin looked at her. "Are you worried more about protecting him? Or yourself?"

Michelle's eyes slid away again. "You're right. I'm such an idiot. I just wanted an adventure. Some excitement. To feel like a *woman* again. You don't know what it's like, being... being a stay-at-home mom. And up until I freaked out, everything was just incredible, Erin. This guy... he's something else."

Erin nodded. "I get it, Shelley. But we don't get to do everything we want."

"You did. You got your bad boy."

"Yeah, and he got shot in the middle of my goddamned living room!" Erin snapped. "Both of us almost died, Shelley. So yeah," she went on in a lower voice. "I got him. But it wasn't easy and we've paid for it every step of the way. Because actions have consequences and love doesn't change that. You know how many bodies I stand over who were killed by people they loved?"

Michelle's shoulders shook and she started to cry again.

"Hey," Erin said, and now she did put out a hand. "I didn't mean to go all self-righteous on you. And Sean's not going to kill you. I know my brother. He'd never hurt you. It'll be okay. You went right up to the edge, but you didn't step over it, and that's something. Your family is what you thought of. That's what's important. So think of them again. Do what you have to for them. There's nothing I wouldn't do for my family."

She thought of something Carlyle had once told her, hearing his angry, tormented voice in her memory. *When it comes to the people I love, there's no bloody line!* Where was her own line? She hadn't found out yet, and for that she was grateful.

"I should go home," Michelle said, once she had her waterworks back under control. "I told Sam I'd be there half an hour ago. She's going to be worried."

"Just slip her an extra twenty for the overtime," Erin suggested, getting to her feet. "She'll be fine."

"Thanks for listening," Michelle said as they walked out of the shop. "You're a good sister. And you're right. I'm not going to lose my family. Not over this, not over anything."

She put her arms around Erin and gave her a tight, fierce hug that had desperation in it. Erin returned the embrace. As she did, she saw a parked car across the street suddenly start up and angle into the road. Two men were in it, the driver and a big, bulky guy in the passenger seat. It was too dark to see their faces. A jolt of irrational alarm shot through her and she pulled back from Michelle, dropping her hand to the butt of her Glock. But the car just drove into the night, of course. It wasn't an assassin, it was just a couple of guys going home after a late night. Erin felt foolish and paranoid.

"Goodnight, Shelley," she said. But she didn't think either of them would be getting any more sleep that night.

Chapter 2

Erin was right. She and Rolf got back to the Corner a little before three. She marched straight to the bar and signaled the bartender.

"Double shot of Glen D, Danny," she said.

"Everything all right, darling?" Carlyle asked quietly. He'd seen her come in and was standing at her elbow.

She raised a hand, one finger up, silently telling him to wait. She snatched up the glass Danny set in front of her, raised it to her mouth, and gulped down two full shots of whiskey. It was like taking a mouthful of fire that burned all the way down. She choked, gasped, and held her mouth open, just breathing for a moment.

"Lord love you, darling, but that's fine top-shelf whiskey you're guzzling," Carlyle said. "Try to show at least a little respect."

Erin shook her head. "You don't know what the hell I've just been hearing," she said. "It's a two-shot night. Or morning. Where's the line between night and morning?"

"I think once you wake up, it's morning," he said.

"Morning, then. For me. I guess for you it's still night."

He smiled. "Aye, that's so. Is this something I ought to be concerning myself with?"

"No. Just family drama. Everyone's going to be fine. I think."

"Grand. Will you be going back to bed? I was thinking of heading that way myself."

"I can't sleep. Not now."

He leaned in closer and pitched his voice low. "I didn't say a word about sleeping, darling."

"Well," she said. "Since you put it that way..."

They'd taken just a couple of steps toward the apartment door when a familiar voice came from behind them.

"Not running off, are you? And here's me just getting here. I hate being late to the party!"

"Don't you ever sleep, Corky?" Erin asked.

"Says the lass who's standing in front of me, fully clad and awake, on the dot of three?" James Corcoran shot back. Carlyle's best friend grinned at her, his green eyes sparkling with mischief.

"I had a family emergency," she said. "What's your excuse?"

"I'd a date," he said. "But don't tell me you're leaving."

"Aye, lad, we are," Carlyle said. "I'll see you tomorrow."

"I hate to be the bearer of bad news," Corky said. "But it's already tomorrow."

"Why don't you go talk to Caitlin?" Erin suggested. "Unless you're all used up for one night?"

"Now that's a grand plan," he said. He winked at her, patted Carlyle affectionately on the shoulder, and moved off.

"The lad's come fresh from a date and you're fobbing him off on one of my waitresses?" Carlyle asked with a raised eyebrow. "You think that's proper?"

"It's Corky," she said, and it was her turn to wink. "Proper's got nothing to do with it."

*   *   *

Erin had hoped to tire herself out, release some stress, then maybe catch a couple hours of sleep before her shift started. Unfortunately, things didn't work out that way. She and Carlyle made a solid effort at wearing one another out, and it was certainly enjoyable, but when they inevitably came down from their peak, he wound up fast asleep and she was lying on her back, staring at the ceiling, thinking and worrying.

She lay there until almost five, then gave up and quietly got out of bed, being careful not to disturb her slumbering lover. She put on her running clothes, which Rolf liked almost as much as her work clothes. Then she let herself out of the apartment, crossed to the parking garage, loaded herself and her K-9 into her unmarked black Charger, and drove to Central Park.

She had a particular jogging route at the southern end of the park. She did some stretches, let Rolf relieve himself, and then started running. The repetitive rhythm of her sneakers on the path gradually chipped away at her tension. So her brother and his wife had some marital problems. So what? No relationship was perfect. They'd work it out. And Michelle hadn't quite had an affair. Technically.

Would her brother see it that way? She didn't know. She and Sean Junior didn't tend to talk about their relationships. Maybe she should tell him. That would pretty much guarantee Michelle would never trust her again.

By the end of her first circuit, in spite of everything, she was feeling pretty good. As she passed the statue that marked the start of her run, deciding she had time for a second loop, a young man fell into stride beside her. He was about average height, very physically fit. He sported a military-style buzz cut, several visible scars, and an intricate Biblical tattoo that ran from his left wrist all the way up under the sleeve of his olive T-shirt.

"Morning, Ian," she said, recognizing Carlyle's driver and bodyguard.

"Ma'am," he predictably replied. Despite her best efforts, he was reluctant to use Erin's name. The former Marine Scout Sniper was unfailingly polite. He was completely reliable, thoroughly professional, and a hardened combat veteran who'd killed dozens of people. Carlyle had once called him the most dangerous man in New York, but Erin always felt safer when he was around.

He didn't ask what she was doing up so early, running before sunrise. Ian felt that other peoples' business was none of his. He just matched her stride for stride, running in companionable silence. With Ian on her right and Rolf on her left, Erin felt about as well-escorted as a woman could be on a morning jog.

When it was over, she offered him a ride back to the Corner.

"No thanks, ma'am," he said. "Got my own transport."

"What're you driving these days? When you're not in Carlyle's Mercedes?"

"Ford Fusion. Gray. Last year's model."

Of course he'd like that car, Erin thought. A nice, inconspicuous one in a neutral color. Something that would blend into the background. "See you around," she said.

"Affirmative, ma'am. We still on for dinner with your brother and his people?"

"Oh, shit," Erin said. She'd forgotten about that. Before any of the other stuff had happened, Michelle had invited her, Carlyle, and Ian to supper, and that was supposed to happen this evening. Ian had made a very good impression on Michelle and the kids, so Shelley had been sure to include him in the invite.

"Problem, ma'am?"

"No. It just slipped my mind for a second." But Erin was

thinking what that dinner was going to be like. If Michelle had told Sean, she could expect lots of frosty silences and maybe a few flying steak knives. If Shelly hadn't, that was even worse. How was she supposed to act? Like everything was fine?

Erin hoped there'd be something juicy waiting for her at Precinct 8, a nice, violent crime to investigate. Murder might be the only thing that could take her mind off the family drama.

*   *   *

"Think fast!"

Erin flinched and reflexively ducked. The crumpled-up wad of paper bounced off her shoulder and landed on the floor. Rolf gave it a cursory sniff, then ignored it.

"Thanks, Vic," she said, walking to her desk. "Don't you have work to do?"

"I'm doing it," Vic Neshenko said, taking another piece of paper out of the file box on his desk and crumpling it into a ball. He launched it at the wastebasket. It hit the rim and bounced off. The big Russian shook his head sadly and tried again. This time he scored a direct hit.

"What're those?" she asked.

"Old DD-5s. They're digitizing the archives. Some smartass thought we ought to take a look and make sure nothing got misfiled. Otherwise it could end up in the wrong part of the database, and I guess civilization would end."

"I think civilization ended back around Y2K," Lieutenant Webb said. "We've been coasting on inertia ever since."

"Like those stars," Vic said. "You know, they burned out years ago, but they're so far away, we still see them shining. You okay, Erin? You look like hell."

"Thanks," she said. "So do you. Are you getting enough sleep?"

"I wish. You know my girlfriend works nights. I gotta wake up early if I want to see her."

"That's new."

"Like hell it is. Zofia's worked the dog watch since before we met. SNEU does ninety percent of their business after hours."

"No, I meant the part about her being your girlfriend."

"I didn't say that," Vic protested.

"Yeah, you did. But the question is, did you mean it?"

He shrugged. "I guess. Maybe. How can you tell if you've got a girlfriend?"

"If you don't know, I can't explain it to you." She turned her attention to Webb. "What've we got cooking today, sir?"

"Zip," Webb said. "Zilch. Nada. Bubkis. It appears Manhattan's wayward souls have reformed their violent lives."

"Which is why I'm going through old Fives," Vic growled. "I think the brass figure if I have to rummage through some other son of a bitch's paperwork long enough, I'll hunt him down and kill him, and then the rest of you will have a homicide to solve."

"What do you need me to do?" Erin asked.

"Right now?" Webb replied. "Nothing."

"Maybe I should give Rolf a training day," she said. "He's due for one. I could use an extra pair of hands, if you can spare Vic."

Vic started to get up, his face brightening. Then his expression changed. "You want those extra hands in bite sleeves, don't you," he said.

Erin grinned at him. "Insights like that made you a Detective."

"And a chew toy," Webb added. "Go on, get out of here, both of you. I'll handle the paperwork for the desk jockeys."

* * *

Normally, Erin would have enjoyed a training day. It was almost like a day off. She and Vic practiced setting Rolf to search for explosives, clear buildings, and take down suspects. It was all fun and games for the K-9, who loved every minute of it. The dog's excitement was infectious. Even Vic, waddling around in the padded bite suit, had to smile at the way the ninety-pound Shepherd grabbed his arm and shook it like a rabbit, tail wagging the whole time.

But Erin's heart wasn't really in it. She kept thinking about Michelle and the upcoming dinner. She was a little sluggish in her commands and she missed several cues with Rolf. She felt tired, but wide awake at the same time, like she used to feel after a long overnight shift on Patrol.

"Erin!" Vic said. He snapped his fingers in her face. "Focus. Hey, where's your head?"

"Sorry. Family stuff."

"Boyfriend?" he guessed. Vic knew all about Carlyle. He even knew the Irishman was secretly an informant, having figured it out on his own. Vic was a lot smarter than he looked.

"No, actually. One of my brothers is having some marital difficulties."

"There's pills you can take for that," he said.

"That's not what I meant. It's not always about sex, Vic."

"So these marital difficulties don't have anything to do with sex?"

She hesitated. Vic smiled triumphantly.

"So who's your brother getting it on with? And which brother? Oh, let me guess. The doc, right? I bet he's got this cute young assistant, just out of nursing school, and they hit the break room at the hospital between shifts. Am I warm or cold?"

"Cold, Vic. Really cold. Like, mid-winter Arctic cold. Sheesh. I wouldn't have pegged you for a daytime soap-opera fan. And stop guessing. I'm not discussing my brother's love life with you."

"Okay, fine. What's it got to do with you, anyway?"

"Nothing. Only I'm having supper at his place tonight."

He whistled. "Copy that. Just make sure you've got your phone with you, in case you need to call in a 10-13. I can alert ESU, have a tactical team on standby."

"That's sweet of you, but I don't think I'll be needing backup. At least, not the kind with guns."

* * *

The first hurdle Erin had to clear that evening was Carlyle. She didn't want to keep him in the dark, and he was good at playing his cards close to the chest, but she also didn't want to show Michelle's dirty laundry to more people than she had to. She settled for telling him their hosts were having a little spat but that she hoped they'd work it out. Carlyle gave her a searching look, but didn't ask any more questions.

The four of them—Erin, Carlyle, Ian, and Rolf—arrived at the O'Reilly house in Midtown around six thirty. The house hadn't turned into a smoking crater. That was promising. Ian hung back, watching the street as his employer climbed the stairs. He wasn't technically on duty at the moment, but Ian Thompson was never entirely off duty, either. If he had an "off" switch, Erin didn't know where it was.

Michelle answered the door. Her smile was as bright as ever, but there was a brittleness in it that put Erin on edge.

"Good evening, Mr. Carlyle," she said. "Erin, Ian. Come on in."

They entered and were immediately met by the pint-sized whirlwind that was Erin's niece Anna. The nine-year-old flung her arms around Rolf's neck and gave the Shepherd a big kiss.

She was already talking about her summer ballet class, skipping straight over the introductory small talk that grownups thought was so important.

Patrick, Anna's younger brother, was shyer. He stood partway up the hall stairs, a plush sheep clutched in one hand, looking solemnly down at the newcomers. The sheep had been a gift from Carlyle and now went everywhere with him. Ian looked up at the boy and gave him a nod and a slight hint of a smile.

To Erin's astonishment, Patrick came down the stairs and, without saying a word, took hold of Ian's leg. For just a second, before he covered it up, Ian's face showed a surprised joy that completely transformed it. The former Marine put a hand on the top of the kid's head in a light, affectionate gesture completely out of character for him.

Patrick had always been a bit of a puzzlement for Erin. Most kids went through a shy stage, but Patrick seemed never to have come out of his shell. Michelle had told Erin she suspected he might have very mild autism, or Asperger's. Maybe, Erin thought, Patrick was attracted to Ian's quiet, competent energy. He was suspicious of adults who came on too strong or too eagerly.

Michelle led her guests into the living room, where Sean Junior was watching ESPN from his favorite chair. He flipped off the TV and stood up to shake hands with the two men. He gave Erin a quick hug and kiss on the cheek.

Erin looked a question at Michelle over her brother's shoulder. Michelle gave a very slight shake of her head, indicating she hadn't told him anything yet. Erin sighed inwardly. This wasn't going to be an easy dinner.

All through the meal, she wondered whether anyone else could sense the tension of untold secrets. She found the talk and laughter superficial and fake to the point of being annoying.

Michelle talked louder than usual, laughed more, and just seemed to be trying way too hard. Sean appeared to be oblivious, or maybe he was just tired. The hospital was working him pretty hard these days. He said they had a staffing shortfall, due to a couple of doctors suddenly taking positions at other hospitals, and the rest of them had to pick up the slack.

"It's extra ER duty for me all this week," he sighed. "And they wonder why so many doctors develop drug dependencies."

"Just say no," Anna advised her dad, drawing general laughter.

Carlyle was his usual cool, pleasant self, saying all the right things. But Erin knew he was watching everybody else, trying to figure things out. She couldn't possibly keep the drama secret from him forever. If she didn't tell him, he was bound to guess.

Ian, on the other hand, was positively glowing. He was more talkative than Erin was used to. It struck her that he'd never had much of a family life of his own. Carlyle had more or less raised him from a street kid, but Carlyle's bachelor lifestyle was very different from what he was seeing here. With the kids and Michelle, especially, he was opening up, letting his guard down. If it weren't for all the drama gnawing at her, Erin would have been moved almost to tears at the sight of the young, damaged former Marine trading grade-school jokes with Anna and meeting Patrick right where he was.

Erin's phone buzzed. She looked at it and saw Webb's name.

"Sorry," she said, pushing back from the table. "I better take this."

She stepped into the kitchen with a feeling of relief, letting the door swing shut behind her for a little privacy. "O'Reilly," she said into the phone.

"Webb here," her commanding officer said. "You'd better get back right away."

"Copy that," she said. "We catch a body?"

"Nobody's dead," Webb said, but something in his tone told her things were very far from all right. "Not yet, anyway."

"What happened, sir?" She thought of hostage situations, impending disasters. Maybe there was a credible threat, a chemical weapon or even a suitcase nuke.

"Mickey Connor's Hummer got blown up about an hour ago," Webb said grimly. "With him in it."

Erin's knees felt suddenly weak and watery. "Where?" she made herself ask.

"Parking garage near a nightclub. The Wild Irish Rose. You know it?"

"I think so. Maybe I should meet you there." She'd heard the name at the Barley Corner, but had never been there. It was a club that fronted for the O'Malleys.

"Good idea. How soon can you be there?"

"Fifteen, maybe twenty minutes."

"Make it fifteen." Webb's said. "You know what this means."

A lisping Daffy Duck voice climbed into the back of Erin's mind from her childhood days watching cartoons. *Of courth you realithe, thith meanth war.*

"Yes, sir," she said. "I'll see you there."

Chapter 3

"I'm sorry," Erin said when she came back into the dining room. "I have to go. Work."

"When they call you, you've got to go," Sean agreed.

"Do you have time for dessert?" Michelle asked. "I'm trying one of your mom's pie recipes."

"I wish," Erin said. "This can't wait. Ian, I hate to pull you away, but you're my ride. Can you give Rolf and me a lift?" As she said it, she gave Carlyle a meaningful look.

"Affirmative," Ian said, getting to his feet. "Ready when you are."

"I'd best go with them," Carlyle said. "My apologies, Mrs. O'Reilly. Thank you for a lovely meal and a grand evening."

"Sorry, kid," Ian said to Patrick. "I've got my orders. Catch you on the flip-side."

"You talk funny," Anna said to Ian. "Did they teach you that when you were a soldier?"

"Marine, miss," he said. "Not soldier."

"What's the difference?"

"Soldiers call for Marines when they need help," Ian said. Then he actually winked at Anna.

After saying their goodbyes, they headed out onto the street. Ian got behind the wheel of Carlyle's Mercedes. Carlyle rode shotgun, while Erin sat in back with Rolf. The engine roared to life and they started rolling.

"How much of a hurry you in, ma'am?" Ian asked.

"Don't break any traffic laws," she said. "But we need to move. You know where the Wild Irish Rose is?"

"Affirmative."

"What's happened, darling?" Carlyle asked. He twisted around in his seat to look at her.

"Mickey Connor's car got blown up. No fatalities."

Carlyle's jaw tightened. "Jesus Christ," he said quietly.

"I have to ask," she said. "Was it you?"

"What?" The word was flat and cold.

"After Mickey went for me, after that card game at Evan's place, you said you'd do this," she said. "You said he'd get in his car one day and have a big surprise."

"I promised you I wouldn't," he reminded her.

"I don't want to believe it was you," she said. "But I have to know."

"Erin, I didn't do this. And I've no notion who did. If that doesn't frighten you, it bloody well should. If someone's planting bombs, I've got to assume they're gunning for all of us. The O'Malleys, I mean."

"Mickey Connor tried to kill you, ma'am?" Ian asked quietly.

"You didn't tell him?" Erin asked Carlyle. She'd assumed he already knew.

"After Mickey tried to frame the lad, I thought it would only add fuel to the fire," Carlyle said. "Ian, I don't want you to go haring off after that gobshite. You understand me?"

"Loud and clear, sir." Ian kept looking ahead. Except for the way his hands clamped a little tighter on the steering wheel, he gave no sign of emotion.

Erin looked into Carlyle's eyes. She saw only honesty and concern. He claimed he'd never lied to her, and never would, but how would she know? She wanted to believe him. Could she trust him?

The hell with that. She'd decided to trust him months ago. This was no time to get cold feet.

"Can you drop me about a block away from the club?" she asked Ian.

"Good thinking," Carlyle said. "It wouldn't do for you to drive up in my car just now. I expect emotions are running a trifle high."

"What would Mickey have been doing at that club?" she asked.

"Don't you know, darling? The Wild Irish Rose is Veronica Blackburn's establishment."

"Oh." That explained a lot. Veronica handled the O'Malleys' narcotics and prostitution. She was a former streetwalker who'd recently taken up with Mickey. This just got better and better.

"Anything else I ought to know going in?" Erin asked after she'd tried to digest that piece of information.

"Just be careful," he said. "And don't expect Mickey to cooperate."

"I expect Mickey to be Mickey," she said. "I expect an obstructive, violent asshole."

"Then you'll not be disappointed."

*　　*　　*

The sun was on its way down, but hadn't quite ducked under the horizon, when Ian pulled over to the curb and Erin unloaded Rolf. A column of black smoke was visible about a block away. Between it and her was a cordon of emergency vehicles, blue and red lights flashing. She saw police cars, a couple of fire trucks, and what looked like the Bomb Squad's van.

"Thanks," she said to Ian. "You guys keep your heads down, okay?"

"Aye," Carlyle said. "And Erin, you may want to take a quick look under your car before you start it, for the foreseeable future."

"Rolf's a bomb-sniffer," she reminded him.

"Best let him have his sniff, then. Ta, darling."

She watched the Mercedes drive away into the gathering dusk. Then she squared her shoulders and walked toward the lights and smoke. Rolf trotted beside her, tail and ears upright, ready for action.

The Wild Irish Rose was a converted warehouse. The nightclub had big, multi-paned windows on the upper floors, painted over to keep out the daylight. Two of those windows, the ones overlooking the parking lot, gaped jaggedly, shards of broken glass hanging from the frames. In the lot, a black Humvee sat drunkenly on one good tire. The shattered wreckage of the big car belched clouds of smoke out of what was left of its engine block. There didn't appear to be an intact windshield or car window within twenty yards of it.

Cops and firefighters were everywhere. Erin picked out several familiar figures at once. She saw Vic, looming above the surrounding officers, and the telltale silhouette of Webb's fedora next to him. They were talking to Skip Taylor, the best bomb tech in the NYPD. And over against the wall of the club stood Mickey Connor.

Erin kept her eyes on Mickey as she approached her commanding officer. It was hard not to look at Mickey. He was enormous, six and a half feet of scar tissue and muscle. He'd put on some weight since his heavyweight boxing days, but it only made him larger and more intimidating. His head was square, his hair cut close to the scalp. His nose and ears showed the lumps gained from years in the ring. He was the most physically terrifying man Erin had ever met. He'd tried to kill her once and come very close to succeeding. She'd have to be crazy to turn her back on him, even in a crowd of New York's Finest. He looked even more the worse for wear than usual this evening. His face was bloodstained and pockmarked with small lacerations.

"What'd I miss, sir?" she asked Webb.

"Hey, Erin," Skip said. "Glad you could join us."

"Taylor was just telling us his initial findings on the explosion," Webb said. "Why don't you start over?"

"Sure thing, Lieutenant," Skip said. "Definitely a car bomb. No doubt whatsoever. I won't know the exact composition of the bomb until I can do some tests on the chemical residue, but looks like ANFO at first glance."

"That stands for..." Webb began.

"Ammonium nitrate fuel oil," Erin said. "I know the stuff. It's what the IRA used in the Troubles."

"That's right," Skip said, smiling at her. "It's easy to manufacture out of everyday ingredients. Fertilizer and fuel oil, mostly."

"That'll make it hard to trace a sale," Vic said gloomily.

"Impossible, if the bomber was smart about it," Webb said. "Our guy probably paid cash and bought the ingredients separately."

"Probably," Skip agreed. "It doesn't appear to have been a very efficient device."

"Why do you say that?" Webb asked.

"For one thing, it's too big," Skip said. "See those broken windows? That's one big-ass blast wave. We saw a lot of car bombs like this in Baghdad when I was in EOD. But those were built for anti-personnel work. They packed nails and ball bearings around them for extra shrapnel. I don't see any shrapnel at all here, except what you'd expect from the car itself."

"Okay, it was big," Webb said. "What else?"

"The guy in the car survived," Skip said. "That's unusual."

"Hold it," Erin said. "Mickey was in that when it went? And he lived?" She pointed to the smoldering wreckage.

"That's one lucky son of a bitch," Vic said.

"Yeah, he was lucky all right," Skip said. "Or maybe the bomber didn't know about that car. It's a damn tank. That thing's got bulletproof windows and armored door panels. I'm guessing the whole crew compartment is armor-plated."

"That's not factory standard," Webb observed.

"Not for a civilian Humvee," Skip said. "But that's no civilian vehicle. That's military surplus with a new paint job. I could take an assault rifle to that thing, point blank, and the guy inside would be just fine. Of course, a bomb this size should've killed him anyway. But our bomber put the damn thing in the wrong place."

"How do you mean?" Erin asked.

"The bomb was under the engine, not the driver's seat. Killed the car just fine, nearly got the driver anyway, but the armor saved him. He took some light damage from spalling, and he probably doesn't hear so good right now, but he'll be okay."

"Spalling?" Erin asked. She'd taken some basic demolitions training when she'd gotten Rolf, but that had been several years ago.

"When a piece of armor, or anything else, gets hit, the force travels through it," Skip explained. "If you hit a piece of metal hard enough, like with a bullet or an explosion, pieces of it fly off the backside. That's called spalling. Those pieces ricochet around, going pretty fast, and tear hell out of whatever they hit. You can die from a missile that doesn't even put a hole in the armor. That's why modern armored vehicles usually have Kevlar lining on the inside. But a big enough blast can still cause it."

"Damn," Vic said. "Somebody really wanted Connor dead."

"Lots of people want him dead," Erin said, leaving out the fact that one of them was her boyfriend.

"So you're saying this bomb matches the MO of the Irish Republican Army," Webb said.

"It's the kind of bomb they used," Skip said. "But lots of people know how to make that sort of bomb. It's not exactly difficult, and it's cheap. That's why the IRA liked the recipe."

"How was it set off?" Erin asked.

"Wired to the ignition, I think. But I need to go through the pieces. Could've been a remote detonator, like a cell phone."

"We'll get the pieces back to your lab as soon as they cool enough to transport," Webb said.

"This pyromaniac here told New York's Bravest not to hose down the car," Vic told Erin. "So they're letting it burn itself out."

"I don't want evidence getting washed away," Skip said. "And chemical extinguishers are a pain in the ass when I'm looking for explosive residue."

"Anything else you can tell us?" Webb asked.

"Not until I take a closer look."

"Then let's talk to our witness," Webb said heavily.

"Why's he even here?" Erin asked. "Mickey hates cops. I'm surprised he hung around."

"He didn't have much choice," Vic said with a smirk. "First responders found him when they got here. He was unconscious, still sitting in the driver's seat. He's lucky he didn't burn to death."

"Or asphyxiate," Webb added. "I don't think he'll want to tell us anything. But we need to try."

*　　*　　*

Erin reminded herself not to show fear when she faced Mickey. She was an NYPD detective, armed, with a trained K-9 and a whole lot of other officers on scene. There was no rational reason to be afraid of him.

But fear was rarely rational. The look Mickey gave her when the squad approached him made her guts go watery. His pale eyes wrote murder across her face. But he didn't say anything, didn't move an inch. Blood was trickling down his cheek from a gash next to his left eye. He appeared completely unaware of it.

"Mr. Connor," Webb said. "I'm Lieutenant Webb from Major Crimes."

Mickey's gaze remained fixed on Erin. They might have been the only two people on Earth.

"Mr. Connor?" Webb repeated. "Can you hear me?"

"Could be he's deaf," Vic said. "You heard what Skip said. A bomb that big goes off next to you, you're lucky if you don't have permanent damage."

"The man asked you a question, Mickey," Erin said without raising her voice.

"I heard him," Mickey growled. His voice was hoarser than usual, probably from smoke inhalation.

"Do you have any idea who might have planted the bomb?" Webb asked.

"Yeah," Mickey said, holding Erin's stare. "I got an idea."

"Who?" Webb pressed.

"It don't matter to you," Mickey said, still refusing to look at anyone else. "And you guys ain't gonna do nothing about it."

"It's our job," Webb said. "Withholding evidence in a felony investigation is a serious matter."

Now Mickey did spare Webb a quick, contemptuous glance. Even Vic looked a little embarrassed. That had been a weak threat and everybody knew it. Mickey was a deeply unpleasant person, but he was, technically speaking, the victim of a crime.

"Mr. Connor," Webb tried again. "It's our job to protect New York City and everyone in it. That includes you. If you don't tell us who tried to kill you, they're going to try again. Next time, they might try harder. Do you want to die?"

"This ain't your problem," Mickey said. "Walk away."

"If you're thinking of street justice," Webb said, "forget about it. Because then you'll be just another criminal and you'll go down too."

"Who's gonna take me down? You?" Mickey spat. He shifted his attention to Vic. "How about you? You think you could take me in?"

"Love to try," Vic said, not giving an inch. "Just give me a reason, scumbag."

Erin didn't say anything. She was studying Mickey's body language, trying to gauge his intentions and the extent of his injuries. Surprisingly, given the close proximity of the explosion, he seemed almost unharmed. And the way he kept looking at her was making her very edgy.

"Don't even think about it," Webb warned Mickey. "You are not starting a war with some other gangster and you're sure as hell not starting one with the NYPD."

"Don't worry," Mickey said. "I ain't gonna hurt him. He'll wish that was all I did by the time I get done. He'll beg me to hurt him."

"What the hell is that supposed to mean?" Erin snapped.

"Figure it out, *Detective*," Mickey said, giving the final word a heavy, sardonic emphasis. "So are you donut-munchers gonna arrest me or not? I got things to do."

"You're not under arrest, Mr. Connor," Webb said. "But don't leave town."

"Oh, I'm staying," Mickey said. "I ain't going nowhere."

"We'll be transporting your car to our station," Webb said. "If you have anything in it you'd like to collect, you can pick it up at Precinct 8. Assuming it hasn't been destroyed and we don't need it as evidence, of course."

"Keep the car," Mickey said. "I got insurance." Without another word, he walked away.

"That guy's a real ray of sunshine," Vic observed.

"We may not have a suspect," Webb said. "But he does. Who do you think he suspects?"

"I thought that was obvious," Erin said softly.

"Me too," Vic said.

Webb put a hand on one hip. "Okay. Who?"

"Carlyle," Vic said. Erin nodded.

"I understand the bomb angle," Webb said, nodding along with them. "But this seems a little sloppy for Carlyle, a little unprofessional."

"If Carlyle had wanted to blow up Mickey, Mickey would be dead," Erin agreed. "This wasn't him."

"We still better get his alibi," Webb said heavily.

"No need," Erin said.

"Seriously, Erin?" Vic said. "I know you like the guy, and I don't think he did it either, but we still need an alibi."

"There's no need because I already know where he was this evening," she said.

"Oh?" Webb was interested. "Where?"

"With me."

"Where?"

"At my brother's house. Having dinner. My brother, his wife, and Ian Thompson can verify it. Assuming you won't just take my word for it," she added with a hint of sharpness.

"Okay, good," Webb said. "That's one name we can cross off the list."

"But someone wants Mickey to think this was Carlyle," Erin added. "Otherwise why use a car bomb?"

"Mickey was supposed to die," Webb said. "Who cares what he thinks?"

"Are you sure about that?" Erin asked.

"Carlyle could've planted the bomb earlier," Vic said thoughtfully.

"I thought you didn't think he did it!" she retorted.

"I don't. I'm just saying it's possible."

"So what's going on here?" Webb asked. "Another O'Malley internal fight? Or someone on the outside trying to make a hit look like a civil war?"

"Could be anyone," Erin said. "Mickey's got a lot of enemies."

"If he thinks it was Carlyle, he might retaliate," Webb said softly.

"I already thought of that, sir," Erin said. "Don't worry about Carlyle. He can take care of himself." She hoped it was true.

"We'll let CSU process the scene," Webb said. "For now, let's get to the Eightball. We'd better start building a timeline and a list of suspects."

"On the plus side, I can pad my resume in case I want a job with a telephone company," Vic said. "Because we're gonna get the damn phone book."

Erin nodded, but her mind was elsewhere. She was staring at the smoking Humvee and trying to think what possible reason there was to set Carlyle and Mickey against one another. Who stood to gain? She had the feeling that if she could figure the motive, she'd have the bomber. But that would take time, and she didn't think Mickey Connor intended to just wait around while the police conducted their investigation. At that moment, she was very glad Carlyle had Ian watching his back.

Because Mickey Connor didn't care who the police thought had tried to kill him. He had his own plans and his own agenda.

So far, no one had died. But unless they were smart and lucky, that wasn't going to be true for long.

Chapter 4

"How'd you get here, anyway?" Vic asked. Erin and Rolf were crammed into the back of his Taurus, behind the mesh. Webb was up front.

"Hitched a ride," Erin said.

"Carlyle?" Vic guessed.

"Yeah."

"And he didn't want to get spotted at the scene," Webb said. "Smart. But I don't think anyone's ever accused him of being dumb."

"You think we ought to question him?" Vic asked. "You know, for the appearance of the thing?"

"I've got a better idea," Erin said. "Why don't we bring him into the Eightball and have him take a look at the bomb?"

"I was being serious," Vic said.

"So was I."

"No," Vic said. "No way. You aren't considering this, are you, sir?"

"It's not a terrible idea," Webb said.

"That's exactly what it is," Vic said. "It's the worst idea in the history of bad ideas. This could taint the whole case!"

"How?" Erin shot back. "He's got no criminal record in the States."

"Yeah, and in Ireland he's a terrorist!"

"He's got amnesty," she said. "The Good Friday Accords..."

"Don't mean a damn thing!" Vic snapped. "If you get a pardon, you still did the crime. A pardoned criminal is still a criminal. If it gets out that we let a professional bomb-maker into Skip's lab, we'll never hear the end of it."

"One thing at a time, people," Webb said. "We have a resident bomb expert and he's as good as they get. Let's see what Skip makes of this."

"Vinnie the Oil Man," Erin said suddenly.

"What about him?" Vic asked.

"The Lucarellis have been getting into it with the O'Malleys for months," she said. "This could be an escalation."

"Yeah, I could see that," Vic said. "If Vinnie Moreno decides to take the O'Malleys down for good, it makes sense for him to go after their muscle first. Sort of like when Luca Brasi gets whacked in *The Godfather*. He's this big dude, everyone's scared of him, but the Tattaglias take him down and he never even sees it coming. Knife in the hand, rope around the neck, bam!"

"Okay, so we're using Mob movies from the Seventies to guide our investigation," Webb said. "That's comforting."

"Hey, mobsters watch those movies, too," Vic said.

"Don't get me wrong, it's a decent theory," Webb said. "Neshenko, O'Reilly, you have contacts in SNEU. Find out what's going on with the Lucarellis."

The Lucarelli Family was an old-school Mafia organization with its primary focus in the narcotics trade. Vic's girlfriend was an officer in the Street Narcotics Enforcement Unit. He and Erin had worked with that unit on several cases and were on good terms with them.

"They should be coming on duty soon," Erin said.

"Yeah, at eight," Vic said. "I'll give Zofia a call."

*   *   *

At the Precinct 8 station, the detectives went upstairs to Major Crimes. While Vic got on the phone with his girlfriend, Erin started setting up the whiteboard. It was a little unusual for Major Crimes to be investigating a case in which no one had been killed. Attempted murders weren't a high priority for their division. But Erin dutifully went to work on the board, writing out what little they had.

They had a victim, a weapon, a time, and a place. So far, that was about it. They were guessing the motive was business, not personal, but that was just because Mickey Connor's business was crime. For all they knew, maybe he had a jealous girlfriend. Or it could be revenge for something Mickey had done. Without motive, it was very hard to identify the correct suspect.

"Good news," Vic announced. "Zofia's squad is running vertical patrols in an apartment complex tonight. She said we can catch them before they hit the first building if we leave now."

"Okay, you two go meet with them," Webb said. "I'll hold the fort here and do some background on the O'Malleys."

So they got right back in Vic's Taurus. This time Erin rode shotgun. Rolf stayed in back.

"Where's your car?" Vic asked.

"Parked across from the Barley Corner," she said.

"Remind me, what's Carlyle drive?"

"He doesn't. He says he tends to forget and drive on the wrong side of the road."

"You know what I mean. What does he ride around in?"

"Mercedes."

"Is his ride armor-plated like Connor's?"

"I don't think so. That Hummer probably got shit for gas mileage."

Vic snickered. "You're not kidding. Gallons per mile, you think? But your boy better take some precautions, especially if he's not riding in a damn tank."

"He's careful."

"He's also been shot a couple times."

"I know," she said sharply.

"Sorry," Vic muttered. "You worried about him?"

"A little."

"Hey, no worries. We'll catch whatever loser is planting bombs, we'll throw his ass in jail, and everything'll be fine. Personally, I'm hoping it's Vinnie. I'd love to slap the cuffs on that slick son of a bitch."

"I don't really see the Oil Man crawling around under cars," she said doubtfully.

"One of his people, then."

"You know how hard it is to pin low-level crimes on mob bosses," she said.

"Hey, how long is this thing gonna go on with you?" he asked.

"You asking me if I'm going to break up with Carlyle?"

"No, I mean the other thing."

"You know we can't talk about that," she reminded him.

"Just tell me this. Is it gonna be over soon?"

"I hope so," she said, looking out the window at the Manhattan streets.

*   *   *

They found the SNEU team outside an apartment tower on the Lower East Side, looking more like a heavily-armed street gang than an organized squad of police officers. SNEU had a reputation as wild cards, and since most of their operations were done in plainclothes, designed to blend in with bad neighborhoods, their hair and clothing was definitely non-regulation. If not for their body armor, and the fact that she knew their faces, Erin would've pegged them as suspicious characters.

Sergeant Logan raised a hand in greeting. The streetlight's reflection glittered on a diamond pinky ring. Logan wore a very tattered leather jacket and had his shield strung on a gold chain around his neck in the time-honored street cop style.

"Hey, nice of you to join us," he said. "We can use a couple extra pairs of boots."

"I've already got a job, but thanks," Erin said. She looked around at the others. "Piekarski, Janovich, Firelli. How you feeling, Firelli?"

Firelli grinned. "Top of the line, O'Reilly. Never better." A little guy with a pencil mustache, he'd been badly wounded earlier that spring in a botched drug bust.

"He just came back to full duty yesterday," Zofia Piekarski said. She favored Vic with a warm smile. "He's maybe not up for the really physical stuff yet."

"Bullshit," Firelli said. "I can kick your ass up one stairwell and down the other, *michelina.*"

"We're here about the Lucarellis," Erin said to Logan.

"Okay, but let's move while we talk," he said. "We've got a lot of ground to cover tonight and I'm serious. A few extra hands will help, just in case things get dicey. Don't worry, we're not planning any takedowns. We're just showing the flag tonight. Watch commander said we've been getting a lot of gang complaints in this area, so this'll show the good citizens we're taking things seriously."

"So it's a PR job?" Vic asked.

"Pretty much," Logan said. "Gotta love departmental politics. But you never know when things are gonna go sideways."

They went into the lobby as a group. Their guns were holstered, but all the officers were alert and aware. A small group of loitering teens by the elevator scattered into the hallways. The cops started up the south stairwell. A vertical patrol was exactly what it sounded like. The officers moved up a high-rise building floor by floor, making sure no obvious criminal activity was going on.

"What do you want to know about the Lucarellis?" Logan asked.

"Somebody tried to whack the chief O'Malley enforcer this evening," Erin said. "We think the Oil Man might be behind it."

"You say they tried," Logan said. "I assume that means they didn't succeed?"

"Mickey Connor's a hard man to kill," Erin said grimly.

Logan thought it over. Janovich shouldered open the door to the second-floor hall. The corridor was deserted. They continued on up.

"Could be," Logan decided. "A couple Lucarelli associates got beat down by Irish guys earlier this week. Word on the street is, the O'Malleys have been testing the border of Little Italy. The Italians might've decided to retaliate. What'd they use?"

"Car bomb."

"And he lived through it? What happened, premature detonation?"

"I knew a guy whose girlfriend broke up with him 'cause he had a problem with that," Janovich put in.

Piekarski choked back a laugh as they reached the third floor landing. It was her turn to open the door. She did. Again, they saw nothing untoward.

"The car was armored," Erin explained.

"Oh, like DeNiro in *Casino*," Firelli said. "Metal plate under the seat save his bacon?"

"Something like that."

"Vinnie's probably pissed at the Irish," Logan said. "But you'll never prove it was him. Not unless you flip one of his guys. I know *omerta* ain't what it used to be, but these guys won't roll over on Vinnie. He's old-school. They know he'll have 'em killed if they even think about snitching. I think it's only a matter of time before he takes over for Old Man Acerbo."

Logan was referring to the titular head of the Lucarellis, currently serving a very long RICO sentence in federal prison. Vincenzo Moreno was only the acting head of the family, but Logan was probably right. Vinnie was the boss in all but name.

"Maybe this is his power play," she said. "Hit the O'Malleys hard and establish a reputation."

Logan nodded. "They've been moving a lot of shit on the street lately," he said. "Heroin and fentanyl mostly, but some meth too. Marijuana, of course, but nobody gives a shit about Mary Jane anymore. We get any of that when we bust the dealers, we just throw it away these days. Not worth prosecuting. Only place the Department draws a line is that we can't smoke it ourselves."

"How do you think we can get to Vinnie?" she asked.

"Make an appointment," Logan said. "I mean that. Call him and set up a meeting."

"He won't tell us a thing," she said.

"Of course not. But you can judge his reactions, maybe see if you're on the mark. That way you'll know whether you're wasting your time with him."

Erin considered. Vinnie probably would talk to her if she asked. They'd struck a bargain in the past, made a deal that had benefitted both the Lucarellis and the NYPD. It had left a bad taste in her mouth, but that was the price of doing business sometimes.

"I'll do that," she said. "You got his phone number?"

He laughed. "No, but he's in the directory. After all, he's a good, upstanding citizen. Totally legitimate. Why wouldn't you be able to reach him?"

"You think he's still awake?"

Logan paused at the next door. "You kidding? He's the same as the rest of us. His workday's just getting started." He shoved the door open. Then his calm, relaxed demeanor instantly changed.

"Hey!" he shouted. "NYPD! Freeze!"

A pair of young men stood staring, like startled rabbits. One was wearing a backpack over one shoulder. For just an instant, nobody moved. Then the one with the pack grabbed his buddy and shoved him into the middle of the hallway. The other kid lost his footing and tumbled to the floor. The one with the pack spun on his heel and sprinted for the opposite stairwell.

The SNEU team poured into the hallway, drawing their guns. Logan was in the lead, Piekarski and Janovich right behind. Firelli lagged a little and Erin noticed him press a hand to his shoulder. He might have been cleared for duty, but he wasn't quite a hundred percent. Logan got tangled with the perp on the floor and the two of them went down in a struggling heap. Piekarski and Janovich clambered awkwardly over them and kept going, while Firelli stayed to help his boss.

Erin hadn't thought anything could surprise her after twelve years wearing a shield, but the quick, almost thoughtless way the one guy had sacrificed the other just to buy himself a couple of seconds took her aback. She glanced at Vic and saw him already going back down the stairs they'd just climbed. She understood at once. The guy Logan's team was chasing might be heading for another stairway, but both sets of stairs led to the same ground floor. She gripped Rolf's leash and followed Vic.

The Russian had longer legs than Erin, but she was quicker on her feet, so they kept pace with each other. Rolf, restrained by his leash, was much faster than either of them, but was forced to stick with his two-legged partners. Neither Vic nor Erin had drawn their sidearms, which turned out to be a good thing. They needed their hands for the railing on the way down. Erin hoped she wouldn't turn an ankle. She thanked her lucky stars that she believed in sensible shoes. Cops in high heels belonged solely to the realm of Hollywood fantasy.

They hit the ground floor running. Vic snatched at the handle and yanked the door open for Erin and Rolf, who barreled straight through. They were halfway across the lobby when the other stairway door flew open and the kid with the backpack sprinted out. He ran for the front entrance. So did Erin and her K-9, angling to cut him off.

The guy was about ten feet away from them when he saw them out of the corner of his eye. An almost comical expression of wide-eyed dismay flashed across his face. He put his head down to keep running.

"*Fass!*" Erin gasped, out of breath from her dash. She let go of the leash.

Rolf wasn't the least bit winded. He'd been hoping for Erin to give him his "bite" command. The Shepherd launched himself forward with his powerful hind legs, overtaking the running human with no apparent effort. His jaws snapped shut on the kid's right arm, pulling him off balance. The fugitive made an inadvertent somersault and landed flat on his back with a tooth-jarring impact.

Rolf didn't have a great grip on the arm, but it was good enough. Erin got there two seconds later. The K-9 looked up at her and wagged his tail, but didn't release his hold. He wouldn't let go until she told him to.

"*Pust,*" she said. Rolf obediently opened his mouth, letting his tongue loll out. The dog was grinning happily.

"Roll over," Erin told the kid. She pulled the pack away, keeping her other hand on her Glock just in case. But Rolf had knocked all the fight out of the suspect. He didn't resist.

"I wasn't doing nothing," he protested weakly.

"Which is why you threw your buddy at us and ran like hell," Erin said dryly. "What's in the pack?"

"It's his, it's not mine," he said, which both was and wasn't an answer.

At that moment, the opposite stairwell door banged open again and disgorged Piekarski and Janovich, guns in hand. Piekarski's face fell when she saw the tableau in front of her. She'd been hoping for more of a chase.

"Good takedown," Vic said from behind Erin. "What's in the pack?"

She unzipped it and showed it to him. The pack contained a couple dozen little plastic baggies of powder.

"Let me guess," Vic said. "Sugar? Cosmetics? No? Ooh, I know, talcum powder! Or chalk dust, maybe?"

"Why'd you come after me, lady?" the guy on the ground complained.

"Because you ran," Erin said. She looked at the two SNEU officers. "How'd Logan know they were dealers?"

Piekarski shrugged. "That's why he's Sarge. He's got the eye."

"Your dog bit me!" the kid whined.

"He didn't even break the skin," Erin said after a quick look. "You're lucky. Shut up and hold still." Janovich produced a pair of handcuffs and snapped the bracelets on their man.

While Janovich and Piekarski collected the perp and the evidence, Erin reached into the pocket of her windbreaker. Rolf followed the gesture intently. He knew what was coming.

Erin drew out a hard rubber Kong chew-toy and tossed it to the K-9. Rolf snagged it in midair and began joyfully working his jaws, chewing the rubber.

"Good boy," she said. "*Sei brav*, Rolf. *Sei brav*."

"Looks like fun, doesn't it," Vic said. "Maybe I should get me one of those."

"It beats cigarettes," Erin said. "We ought to get one for Webb."

Logan and Firelli came down the elevator with the other young man, also in cuffs. One of Logan's cheeks was swollen and discolored, showing the beginning of what promised to be an impressive bruise, but he was smiling.

"Good start to the night," he said. "Anyone recognize either of these guys?"

"That one looks a little like Shifty Diallo," Piekarski said, pointing to the one Firelli was holding.

"The very same," Logan said. "Haven't seen you in a while, Shifty. When did you get back on the street?"

"Two weeks ago," Diallo said.

"And already back at your old tricks," Logan said. "Well, if you're lucky, maybe the boys up at Riker's haven't reassigned your cell yet and you can get your old bed back. Might even still be warm."

"Hey, man, sorry about the face," Diallo said.

"Forget about it," Logan said, patting him on the shoulder. "All part of the game. Not your fault. Your buddy here chucked you under the bus. I blame him."

"They're talking like they're friends," Erin said to Piekarski in an undertone.

"You know how it is," she replied softly. "We're all playing the same game. Our team just won this round. Shifty's been in and out of jail since he was fifteen. He's used to it. He don't take it personal."

"Yeah," Logan said as they walked him out. "And since he didn't have any product on him, he's the smart one. I bet he gets a slap on the wrist and does thirty days, tops. In and out."

"What about resisting arrest?" Vic asked.

"What, this?" Logan pointed to his face. "Nah, that don't count. That was an accident. I tripped over him. Did you guys get what you needed?"

"I guess," Erin said.

"Thanks for the assist," he said. "Catch you later. Drinks at the usual place at six, if you're interested. Firelli's buying."

"We'll see," she said. "I might want to get some sleep tonight."

"Sleep? At night?" Firelli looked appalled. "Who'd ever want to do that?"

Chapter 5

"Well?" Vic asked. "You gonna call the Oil Man, or what?"

They were sitting in Vic's car, parked near the apartment complex. The SNEU squad had departed for their home station, suspects in tow. Erin was staring at her phone. She had Vincenzo Moreno's number entered. It stared back at her, daring her to make the call.

"Yeah," she finally said. But she got out of the Taurus before she hit the green button. Vic watched her put the phone to her ear. He didn't say anything, but he got out of the car and leaned against it, arms crossed.

The phone rang four times and rolled to voicemail. It was one of those impersonal automatic messages, a robotic voice that repeated the number and instructed her to leave a message.

"Hey, Vinnie," she said. "This is Erin O'Reilly. Drop me a line at this number when you get this. We need to talk."

"Paranoid much?" Vic asked. "Seriously, Erin, I could believe somebody might've bugged your ride, but mine, too?"

"I'm making no assumptions," she said, taking a quick look around to make sure no passersby were within earshot. "And

I'm taking this very seriously. You haven't told anybody about... about my situation, have you?"

"Of course not!" He bristled. "You could've trusted me from the start."

"I did... I do trust you. Trust isn't the point. The more people who know, the more likely something is to slip, no matter what our intentions are. Vic, somebody tried to take out Mickey and they're framing Carlyle for it. That puts him in danger."

"That's the ride he signed up for," Vic said.

"And you wonder why I might not have trusted you with this," she said bitterly.

"Hey," he said. "I didn't mean it like that. Are you asking me to like this mope? 'Cause I don't. And I'm not gonna. And if he puts you in the line of fire on account of his goddamn lifestyle, I'm gonna like him a lot less."

"He's getting out of the Life, Vic. The right way."

"Yeah, every gangster's about to get out of the Life. Just like every smoker's about to quit. And every junkie's taking his last shot of heroin. Wake up, Erin. People don't leave the Life."

She shook her head. "You don't understand—" she began.

Her phone, forgotten in her hand, buzzed. Startled, she looked down at it and saw an unknown number. She thumbed it and brought it back up.

"O'Reilly," she said.

"I understand you wanted to talk to me," a smooth, cultured male voice said. "I prefer not to transact business by phone. If it's convenient, I'll be in Little Italy at a café for the next couple of hours. Do you know Giovanni's?"

"I can find it."

"Then I'll look for you. One thing. Please approach in the open, with your hands empty. The street's a little unsettled this evening and we wouldn't want any misunderstandings." The call disconnected.

"I've got a meeting with Vinnie," she announced.

"Great," Vic said. "Let's go."

"It should be just me."

He nodded. "Okay. So, you gonna call a cab, or what? And you want the taxi guy to be your backup if things go sideways?"

Erin had to smile. "Okay, fine. You can come, but he won't talk to the both of us. You'd better keep your distance."

"You're assuming he'll talk to you."

"He wouldn't have gone to the trouble of setting up a meet if he didn't have something to say."

"It'll be bullshit."

"I know that, Vic. These guys are liars. But if you sift through the bullshit, sometimes you find something useful."

He made a face. "I try not to stick my hands in the stuff. If I wanted to shovel shit all day, I'd have been a farmer. Just be careful, okay? These mopes are dangerous."

"Vinnie's not going to kill a cop."

"You willing to bet your life on that?"

"Mine? No. Yours? Now there's a thought. Maybe it's a good thing you'll be there after all."

"Bite me, O'Reilly."

* * *

Giovanni's was a pleasant little mom-and-pop café with a cheerful red awning. As she walked Rolf through the front door, Erin noted the clientele was skewed toward serious-looking young Italian men. All of them were wearing loose outer shirts or coats that could easily be hiding weapons.

"You still like this?" Vic asked in an undertone.

"It's fine," she said through clenched teeth. "Just stay near the door and keep your eyes open and your hands empty."

Vic didn't like it, but he peeled off from her and took up a position just to the side of the door, from which he exchanged stares with a pair of hard-faced goons. Erin continued into the café, aiming for a booth near the back. She couldn't see the booth's occupant, but two more thugs had pulled chairs across the floor to block easy access, so she figured it was a good bet. One of them, in spite of the mild June weather, was wearing a long black coat. Both men stood when she approached. One had his hand in his pocket. The other reached under the flap of his coat.

"Take it easy," she said, making sure to keep her hands in plain view. "I'm just here to talk." Rolf eyed the men. His hackles were up, his ears flattening against his skull. The Shepherd didn't know exactly what was going on, but he could feel the nervous energy in the room and didn't like it.

"It's fine, boys," said the man in the booth. "She's here by invitation. And don't bother frisking her. We all know she's carrying, and she won't be surrendering her iron to the likes of you."

The guy in the trench coat started to protest, but he thought better of it, shut his mouth, and moved aside. Erin walked past the bodyguards and turned to face Vincenzo Moreno.

The acting head of the Lucarelli Mafia family got to his feet and offered his hand. He was a slickly handsome man of about fifty, his hair jet black and combed back in the classic gangster style. He was immaculately and expensively dressed in a pinstriped suit and scarlet necktie. The hand he extended was clean, nails neatly trimmed, and a pair of rings glittered on the third and fourth fingers. His smile had as much warmth as a meat locker. His eyes were glossy black marbles, like a shark's.

Erin shook hands briefly and took a seat opposite Vinnie. "Thanks for meeting me, Mr. Moreno," she said. Rolf, seeing her sit, settled himself just outside the booth and stared at her, waiting for instructions.

Vinnie sat back down. "My pleasure," he said. "Can I get you anything? The focaccia is excellent. Or maybe just a cup of coffee?"

"Coffee, thanks," she said. "Cream, no sugar."

Vinnie nodded to one of his guys. "Nicky, if you'd be so kind?"

The man jumped up and went quickly to the counter.

Erin reminded herself to be normal, as relaxed as possible. She was wearing a concealed recording wire, courtesy of Phil Stachowski's undercover unit's technicians. It was sewn into her bra's underwire, which was a little creepy but practical. Phil had warned her that her own body language was more likely to give her away than the technology itself.

"You heard about Mickey Connor," Erin said. It wasn't a question.

"Now why would you say that?" Vinnie asked. Both of them were looking into the other's eyes, reading each other, probing for information.

"You hear things," she said. "Besides, you always have one or two guys on you. Tonight you've got four and they're jumpy as hell. You're expecting trouble."

"That's an interesting inference," Vinnie said.

"Do you have an alternate explanation?"

He was still smiling. "I'm a superstitious man," he said. "My horoscope warned me to be on the lookout for unexpected visitors. I can't help but notice you didn't come alone, either."

"I guess we're both superstitious," she said, trying to give nothing away. "The hit on Mickey was botched."

"Really?" Vinnie said, raising a polite eyebrow. "What makes you so sure?"

"I talked to him after. He's pissed, but he's still very much alive."

"I heard something on the news, now that you mention it," Vinnie said. "A car exploded, if I heard correctly."

Vinnie wasn't guessing. He knew exactly what had happened, whether he was behind it or not. He and Erin both knew that. He was hardly even trying to pretend otherwise.

"The bomber screwed up," Erin said. "Mickey wasn't badly hurt. You don't need to worry about me, Mr. Moreno. You need to worry about him."

"I'd only need to worry about him if I was responsible," Vinnie said mildly. "Thanks, Nicky," he added as his goon placed a cup of coffee in front of Erin.

"That's not quite true." She took a sip. It was a good, expensive brew, but she hardly noticed the taste. "You need to worry if he *thinks* you're responsible."

Vinnie inclined his head to indicate she had a point. "And is that why you're here? To negotiate a cessation of hostilities before a bunch of gangland hotheads start making more work for your department?"

She shook her head. "I'm just trying to find the truth."

"You say that like it's a simple thing," Vinnie said. "It's a slippery concept, truth, hard to hold onto. Even if you manage to grab onto it, you may not like what you've got in your hands."

"What's that supposed to mean?" she demanded. It was a weak question, one she didn't really expect him to answer, and he didn't.

"I'm a man who's good at getting what, or who, he wants," Vinnie said, looking right into her eyes. "I have no fondness for Mickey Connor. You know him as well as I do. He's a psychopathic murderer, a sadistic man who delights in hurting people. I also know that he's a vindictive man. In my line of work, Detective, some of us still hold to an older, more honorable code. We would never think of involving civilians in any unpleasantness. My wife and children, for instance, are entirely off-limits. Mr. Connor has no such compunctions. If he wants to hurt someone, he will do whatever he calculates will cause the most pain and distress. I have no wish to pick a fight with such a man. The collateral damage would be... unacceptable."

"The bomber wasn't looking to pick a fight," Erin said. "He was looking to kill him."

"I wonder," Vinnie said. "People do, on occasion, survive such things. But it's rare and usually requires the perpetrator to commit some sort of blunder. Does my reputation suggest to you, Detective, that I am a blunderer?"

"No, it does not," Erin said.

"Then it would be reasonable to conclude, would it not, that I did not want to kill Mr. Connor at this time and place?"

"That sounds reasonable," she said warily.

"Excellent. Then we understand one another. Besides, what would I possibly stand to gain?"

"You'd eliminate a rival's chief enforcer," Erin said. "You'd weaken the O'Malleys."

"Nonsense. Mr. Connor has particular talents, but they're very limited. What he brings is primarily a violent mindset, a willingness to do terrible things. I'll admit, that's a useful sort of man for certain activities, but such men are replaceable and, therefore, ultimately expendable. A man like your Mr. Carlyle, on the other hand, is much more difficult to replace."

Erin felt a shiver run down her spine. She had no doubt that Vinnie was quite capable of ordering Carlyle's death, or even of killing him with his own hands if necessary. "He's a hard man to get rid of," she said.

"Some men are difficult to remove," Vinnie said. "But if the will is strong enough, there's always a way. How is Mr. Carlyle, by the way? I've heard he's fully recovered from his injuries."

"He's fine," Erin said, her jaw clenched. She tried to speak in a relaxed tone. "You'd never know he'd been hurt."

Vinnie smiled icily. "Excellent. I can only imagine how trying these past weeks have been for you, how worried you must have been. Do give him my regards. Tell him I'm thinking of him. Often."

"I'll pass that along."

"Thank you for stopping by, Detective. I'm sorry I can't be of more assistance in your present difficulty. I look forward to our continued acquaintance."

Erin got up. As she stepped out of the booth, she paused. "One more thing," she said.

"Oh?"

"Shifty Diallo got pinched again, along with one of his buddies. I expect you'll be hearing from him once he gets his phone call."

She left Vinnie with that parting shot, not bothering to look back.

*　　*　　*

Vic tailed Erin out of the café and fell in step beside her and Rolf. He did take a glance over his shoulder.

"Last time I saw that many wiseguys in one place, I think it was Riker's Island," he said. "And they've got enough hardware in there for an NRA convention."

"They're spooked," she said.

"Vinnie give you anything?"

"He didn't say no and he didn't say yes."

Vic snorted. "I don't want to say I called it, but I did. All bullshit."

"I don't think so," she said.

"So he's our guy?"

She shook her head. "He implied that if he'd wanted to kill Mickey, Mickey would be dead."

"Of course he said that. These guys are all about image."

"He also said Mickey was expendable."

"So Connor's not worth his time?"

"Pretty much. He doesn't seem to respect Mickey very much."

"I don't respect him either," Vic said. "Never thought I'd agree with Vinnie the Oil Man. Can you convince me this wasn't a waste of time?"

"I don't know." Erin was running the conversation through her memory. Later, she could replay it word for word off the wire if she needed to. "He had some things to say, but you have to read between the lines. Translating, he said if he wanted a war with the O'Malleys, he'd go after a higher-value target."

"Like your boyfriend?" Vic said it half-jokingly.

"Exactly," she said, not joking at all. "He also suggested maybe the point of the bomb wasn't to kill Mickey, unless the bomber was a complete incompetent."

"These guys aren't Mensa candidates," he said. "And car bombs don't always work. There's Frank Rosenthal in Vegas. You know, the guy they based de Niro's *Casino* character on? And Danny Greene in Cleveland survived a car bomb *and* a house bomb."

"The second car bomb got him, though," Erin said. As an Irish cop, she knew all about Danny "The Irishman" Greene, the mad-dog mobster who'd taken on the Cleveland Mafia in the Seventies single-handed and nearly won. He'd lost when the Mafia had tapped his phone, tracked him to a dentist's appointment, and blown up the car next to Greene's via remote control.

"Yeah," Vic said. "But my point is, both those guys had Mafia hitmen plant bombs in their cars. Those bombs went off, while they were in the cars, and they both lived. Maybe Connor's just lucky."

"We still need a motive," Erin said.

"Who the hell cares? Connor isn't exactly benefitting society. If some other lowlife wants to whack him, why don't we just let them take out the trash?"

Erin stopped just outside her car and put a hand on her hip. "Do you have any idea how big that bomb under Mickey's car was?" she demanded. "Suppose he'd been parked outside a shopping center? Or a coffee shop? Or a preschool? It's a miracle no bystanders were close enough to get killed this time. You want to talk about lucky? What do you think happens next time? Even assuming you're willing to sit back and let murderers kill people, whoever they are."

Vic lowered his eyes and cleared his throat. "Yeah, you're right. Obviously we've gotta stop them if we can."

"Plus, Mickey's going to be on the warpath himself now," she pressed.

"Okay, okay, Erin. You made your point. What now?"

Erin's next words weren't directed toward Vic. "Rolf? *Such!*" she said, pointing to Vic's Taurus.

The K-9 went into his search mode, snuffling at the wheel wells, circling the car. He made a full circuit with Erin. Then he looked up at her and wagged his tail.

"Okay, we're clear," she said. "Let's get out of here. Take me to the Barley Corner."

"Jesus Christ," Vic said quietly. "You think someone's gonna plant a bomb under a police car?"

"Better safe than sorry."

"We were in there for, like, fifteen minutes!"

"Still."

"If I'm gonna keep being your chauffeur, I want hazard pay," he said, climbing in and starting the engine. "This is how you live?"

"This is what keeps me alive," she corrected.

"You sure you don't want to go back to the Eightball?"

"No, take me home. I've got gangsters to talk to."

"Oh, good. Much safer."

Chapter 6

"I can come in with you if you want," Vic offered.

"That's sweet of you to walk me home after school," Erin said. "Are you going to beat up the bullies on the playground, too? I live here, remember?"

"Hard to forget. I'm going to the Eightball, gonna see what I can dig up."

"Good night, Vic."

"Catch you on the flip-side. Don't get shot."

She watched him drive away from the Barley Corner. Then she squared her shoulders and went in. She was expecting pretty much the same thing she'd just come from at Giovanni's: an armed camp. What she found was a party.

The first person she saw was James Corcoran. Corky was a small man, only a little taller than Erin, but at the moment he was head and shoulders above everyone else in the room. He was standing on top of a table, his red curls almost brushing a ceiling fan, arms akimbo, doing an Irish step-dance. A circle of spectators was cheering him on, clapping their hands in time to a very fast Irish folk song playing on of the bar's sound system.

Erin had no idea what to think. Didn't these idiots know what was going on? Her confusion quickly gave way to irritation. She brushed past the crowd of drunken Irishmen who were singing a song their great-grandfathers had probably brought over from the old country.

Carlyle wasn't there. She didn't see Ian, either, though she did pick out a trio of young men, all sporting military-style haircuts and visible tattoos, in carefully-chosen tactical positions around the pub. That made her feel a little better. At least somebody was on guard. She saw a big glass bowl on the bar, full of punch. Danny was ladling it out to the guests, his hands in more or less continuous motion. To judge by the appreciative response he was getting, it was very strong punch indeed. As she watched, he pulled out a whiskey bottle and upended it over the bowl, pouring in a generous dose of hard liquor.

As she made her way to the back stairs, she wondered at exactly what point it had become comforting to have armed mobsters surrounding her. But then, they weren't exactly mobsters. These were Ian's guys, former military, and probably more trustworthy than most.

She slipped through the armor-plated door, making sure it locked behind her and her dog. "It's me," she called up the stairs.

"I'm in the office, darling," Carlyle called back.

She found him seated at his desk. Ian Thompson stood in front of his employer in a parade rest pose, hands behind his back. The former Marine was wearing a dark gray T-shirt that showed off the intricate tattoo that ran all the way down his left arm. A Beretta nine-millimeter automatic rested in a holster on his right hip. Ian was licensed to carry, but he rarely did it so obviously.

"Am I interrupting something?" Erin asked.

"We were just discussing the best way for Ian to utilize his talents in our present situation," Carlyle said. "You were saying, lad?"

"If I'm covering this position, I'm more effective on overwatch," Ian said. "I've scouted the terrain and I can set up a hide in the garage across the street. I can cover the alley and the front door from there."

"And let us know if anyone tries to shoot their way in?" Erin asked.

"I'll provide cover, ma'am."

"That's a little far for accurate pistol shooting," she said.

Ian nodded and said nothing.

"You want to set up with a *rifle*?" she exclaimed. "In downtown Manhattan? Are you out of your mind? Anyone sees you, they'll call Homeland Security! Or the FBI! We'll have Feds all over the place!"

"They won't see me, ma'am," he said with calm certainty.

"I don't think we've quite come to that eventuality," Carlyle said. "We're not at war, lad. Not yet, at any rate. I'm still thinking the other option is preferable."

"What's that?" Erin asked.

"I can shadow Mr. Connor," Ian said.

"How does that protect you?" Erin asked Carlyle.

"I'm more concerned about Mickey than the Corner at present," Carlyle said. "Haven't you heard?"

"What now?" She braced herself.

"Mickey accosted one of my lads a short while ago. He asked the lad a few questions. When he didn't like the answers, he broke the poor blighter's jaw and dislocated both his arms."

Erin winced. "Where's your guy now?"

"At the hospital, naturally. He's hurting, but he'll recover."

"And the rest of your guys are downstairs celebrating?" she exclaimed in disbelief.

"Of course," Carlyle said mildly. "The logical thing was to get all my lads in the same place, without unduly alarming them. I had Corky collect as many as he could. They're here, being protected. They think it's just a party. It's only lads I trust in the Corner tonight, darling. Or didn't you notice the sign on the door?"

"What sign?" She'd been too preoccupied to read the notice, though now she remembered seeing a piece of paper taped to the front door.

"The pub's reserved for a private event," Carlyle explained.

"Nobody stopped me at the door," Erin objected.

"That's because they know you by sight, ma'am," Ian said. "You had eyes on you the whole time."

"So Mickey's attacking your people?" Erin asked. "Okay. I can arrest him on assault charges. We just need a statement from your guy and—"

Carlyle was already shaking his head. "Nay, darling, that's not how this goes. I've called Evan. He's arranging a sit-down between Mickey and me. We'll have to handle this our way. Bringing coppers into it will only make tempers hotter."

"I'm a copper," she argued. "Cop. Whatever. And busting him will get that son of a bitch off the street."

"Temporarily," he said. "While making the rest of his lads even angrier. One doesn't put out a fire by spraying petrol on it. It's better to smother it."

Erin suppressed a growl of frustration. "When's the meeting?" she asked as calmly as she could.

"Tomorrow at noon."

"Is it in a secure location?"

"Evan's rented the boardroom at a bank."

"Just like *The Godfather*," she said. "He's got a theatrical streak."

Carlyle shrugged. "It's comfortable and safe. I'll have plenty of security to make sure I get there in one piece."

"And you'll have me right beside you."

"I don't think you should be there, Erin."

"Try to stop me."

He smiled. "It's your decision, of course."

"Good, then it's settled. But what's Mickey going to do in the meantime?"

"That's what Ian and I were trying to figure," Carlyle said. "We're fairly buttoned up here. And Mickey's agreed to the meeting, so I think it's unlikely he'll try anything before then. It'd make Evan particularly upset, and I don't think he'll risk it. But in case that's not true, Ian's volunteered to track him."

"Do you know where he is now?" Erin asked.

"Back at the Wild Irish Rose, as of a quarter of an hour ago," Carlyle said.

"I can acquire him there, sir," Ian said.

"Then perhaps you'd best do that," Carlyle said. "It'll make a sleepless night for you, I fear."

"Won't be my first, sir."

Carlyle smiled. "Good lad. Best be about it, then."

Ian nodded once and turned to go. Erin followed him to the top of the stairs.

"Hold on a second," she said.

He paused. "What's up?"

"Don't get in a fight with Mickey," she said.

His expression didn't change. "Won't be a problem, ma'am. This is recon. If this was a combat op, I'd be going a lot heavier. But I don't understand."

"What don't you understand?"

"Mr. Connor tried to take you out."

"He failed."

"He'll try again. He'll keep coming until someone puts him down."

"Ian..." she began. She put a hand on his shoulder. "We can't do shit like that."

"*You* can't, ma'am," he said, placing a very slight emphasis on the first word.

Erin was once again conscious of the impossible position she was occupying. She believed, truly believed, Ian wasn't a bad man. He was, in fact, a very good man. But here was this good, damaged, young former Marine offering to commit murder on her behalf, wondering why she didn't want him to.

"I'm a cop, Ian. If we start going along with that sort of thing, in the end we're just thugs who carry shields. Maybe some guys can live with that, but I can't."

His face was stony. "Forget I said anything, ma'am."

She felt the muscle in his upper arm. It was tense and rigid under her touch. "Ian, we'll get Mickey," she promised. "But not this way. Real justice, not street justice."

"With all due respect, ma'am, there's no such thing. And thank God for that."

"What?" She wasn't sure she'd heard him right.

"If real justice existed, we'd all be fucked," Ian said. He didn't smile as he said it. Erin didn't think he was joking. And she noted his profanity. He didn't swear often, and when he did, it was a sign he was in full-on combat mode.

"What do you mean?" she asked.

"Done some things I'm not proud of, ma'am."

"So have all of us. But we're the good guys. Shit, you're a damn war hero."

It was the wrong thing to say. Erin saw that as soon as the words left her mouth. Ian's face rarely showed expression, but now he was angry.

"You don't know shit about heroes," he said coldly. "Ma'am."

"Is this because of that thing in Afghanistan?" she asked. "Because they gave you a medal you don't feel like you deserved?"

"I'm no fucking hero!" he burst out. "Get that through your goddamn head!"

Erin was genuinely shocked. "Okay," she said, putting up her hands in a calming gesture. "It's okay, Ian."

"No it's not," he said. "You don't get it. I'm glad you don't."

Back when she'd been a Patrol cop, Erin had seen plenty of guys at the end of their emotional tether. Ian was keeping it together better than most, but he was a grenade ready to go off. She couldn't let him take to the street that way. He'd do something reckless and somebody would get hurt. She had to calm him down.

"Talk to me," she said softly. "Help me understand."

He shook his head. "You don't want to know, ma'am."

"You can tell me," she said. "Anything. I promise."

He didn't speak for a while. She watched him wrestling with himself, the man trying to decide. She took his hand in hers, thumb wrapped around his, a warrior's handshake. And she waited. Erin could wait a long, long time when she had to.

"I was in the Sandbox," he said at last. "First tour. They sent me to the 'Stan the second time round, but the first time, I was in Fallujah. Iraq."

"I saw that on the news," she said. "I heard it was pretty bad."

"Bad enough," he said. "I'd just graduated Scout Sniper training. Figured I was pretty badass. Ever seen one of our unit badges? They're black, rifles and skulls on them. They say 'One shot, one kill.' Some of the guys got tattoos to match.

"My unit was doing a lot of house-to-house stuff. We had militants in our sector. Lots of IEDs, guys with suicide vests. I was with a pretty good squad. Couple veterans, the rest of them learned fast. Got my first three kills the first week. All clean shots, just like in training. We took a couple casualties, but no KIAs."

Erin listened carefully. She had no idea where this was going, but she knew better than to interrupt.

"Day nine, we were clearing a residential block," he continued. "All the civvies were supposed to be evacuated. They'd had loudspeaker trucks driving around, terps yelling for everybody to get out."

"Terps?" Erin wasn't well versed in military slang.

"Interpreters. Iraqis who were working with us. Good guys, most of them. A couple jerks, but our terp was solid. What with the broadcasts and the artillery and the airstrikes, we figured all the civvies had booked it and the only guys left were hajjis."

"I'm sorry. Hajjis?"

"Islamic militants. Guys who've been on the hajj. You know, what Muslims are supposed to do. Go to Mecca, run a couple laps around that big black rock?"

"Copy that."

"I'm on sniper overwatch with my spotter, about a hundred meters out," Ian said, shifting to the present tense. Erin had noticed lots of people did this with traumatic memories. Maybe it was subconscious, because what had happened wasn't really in the past for them. "My guys are clearing the third house. We got a fire team stacked up at the door, ready to make entry, and I see someone in a burka. One of those long dresses with a veil over the face. Women wear them, but for all I know, could be anybody under there. Not that it matters. They strap bombs to women, too. She bursts out of the fourth house and starts running toward my squad. And she's holding something in her arms. I'm thinking bomb. ROEs are clear. Anybody charges us in a combat zone, we take them down."

"ROEs?"

"Rules of Engagement. Sorry."

"Forget about it. Go on."

"She's just a few meters from my team," Ian said. He was still looking at Erin, but his eyes had gone distant and she knew he was seeing Iraq. "And I know it's a woman, because I hear her voice. She's screaming something. I hear something about Allah, and I figure she's saying a prayer right before she sets off her bomb. She's going to kill herself and all my guys. I've got a shot, so I take it."

"Sounds like you didn't have a choice," Erin said quietly. She kept her grip on his hand. "But you didn't want to shoot a woman?"

"She goes down," he said, ignoring the question. "Head shot was chancy, so I went for center-of-mass. Sarge goes over to check her. He looks at the package she's holding. Sarge is on his third tour, okay? He's a hardass. I never saw him show anything, not when we're deployed. Face like a block of wood. All of a sudden, he turns away and pukes all over the ground. Then he sits down right there in the dirt, puts his head in his hands. That's when I know something's wrong.

"I'm not supposed to do it, but I get up out of my hide. My spotter asks what the hell I'm doing. I don't say anything, I just know I've got to see what I did. I run over there. Lindy, Private Lindemann, he tries to stop me. He puts an arm around me and says I don't want to see. And I don't want to, but I know I have to. I shove past him and look."

"What did you see?" Erin asked, trying to keep her voice gentle.

"It's not a bomb she's holding," Ian whispered. "She's holding her baby."

"Oh." It was the only thing Erin could think of to say.

"You ever heard of a Quigley?" he asked.

"A what?" She wasn't sure she'd heard correctly.

"A Quigley. It's a sniper thing. There's this movie with this cowboy named Quigley, and he takes a shot with his rifle when there's two bad guys lined up. He hits the first one and gets the second one with the overpenetration. Two for one. That's a Quigley."

"I don't understand."

"It's pretty much impossible," Ian said. "On the battlefield, things never line up right. And even if you get a chance, the bullet tumbles when it hits bone and won't go in a straight line. I'm the only guy I know who ever did it."

She still didn't understand. Maybe she wasn't letting herself.

"I got both of them," Ian said. "The mom and her son. Straight through. Baby wasn't more than three months old. Woman was nineteen, maybe. Just a kid herself."

"Jesus," Erin whispered.

"Sarge said I did the right thing, once he got his shit together," Ian said. "But I knew better. Later on, back at base, I asked the terp what she'd been saying. He didn't want to tell me, but I made him. She was saying, 'Help me, for God's sake.' Innocent girl, begging for help. I killed her. And her kid."

"That wasn't your fault," she said. "You couldn't have known."

"Should've seen. Should've been sharper."

"The tattoo on your arm," she said, suddenly understanding. "You told me you had one done for everybody you shot in the war. Most of them are men, but there's that one figure…"

"Virgin Mary and baby Jesus," he said. "Yeah."

Erin didn't know what to say. Ian turned his eyes back toward her. Now he just looked very, very tired.

"I'm no hero," he said again. "I sometimes figure maybe... It's stupid, but maybe if I could save someone, maybe a kid, it might make up for the others, you know? Like, it might balance the scales or something. But it doesn't work like that, I guess."

Erin just nodded, gave his hand a final squeeze, and let go.

"Will that be all, ma'am?" he asked. And just like that, he was focused on his current mission again. Nobody would have known anything was bothering him.

"Be careful, Ian," she said. "Mickey's dangerous."

"I know, ma'am. So am I. I won't let you down." Then he was gone, leaving her staring after him.

Carlyle looked up as she walked back into his office. "All well, darling?"

"I guess." She sat on the edge of his desk and sighed. "I ordered him not to kill Mickey."

Carlyle blinked. "Not a bad thought. You do know it would solve a great many problems, however."

"Not you too! For the last time, we are not murdering anybody!"

He smiled. "I know, darling. I'm just saying it would be a mite easier."

"Tell me about it. I talked to Vinnie the Oil Man this evening."

"Really?" Carlyle was interested. "And what did Mr. Moreno have to contribute?"

"He indicated he didn't try for Mickey. Oh, and I think he threatened to kill you."

Carlyle seemed neither surprised nor upset. "He's welcome to try," he said mildly.

"Mickey thinks it was you," she said. "Do you really think any agreement Evan pushes him into will keep him in check?"

"It needn't hold him forever," he reminded her. "Just until we finish building our case."

"How long?"

"A few months, probably. We've laid in quite a store of recordings and other evidence. The more we can get, the better."

"Which am I supposed to do?" she wondered aloud. "Find the bomber, or stick to Mickey?"

"Ian will let us know if Mickey does anything," Carlyle said. "Have some faith in the lad. In the meantime, do the job that's in front of you. Believe me, I'm as curious as yourself as to who might have planted the device. And now, I'd best get downstairs and make sure Corky's not causing more trouble than usual."

"I'd better try to get some rest," Erin said. "I'll see what the bomb can tell us. Maybe Skip will have some answers. Wake me up if the world ends, okay?"

"I'd not have you miss it." He kissed her. "Pleasant dreams, darling."

"Yeah, right."

*　　*　　*

To her own surprise, Erin slept through the night, untroubled by nightmares. She did wake briefly when Carlyle came in a little after two, but she got back to sleep again, rising refreshed. She checked the news and the police-band radio as soon as she was up. Nothing seemed to have happened overnight.

She was tense and jittery anyway. Under normal circumstances she would have gone for a run and tried to let out the nervous energy that way, but that seemed like an unnecessary risk this morning. She felt like something was coming. It was like an electricity in the air, the way it felt before a summer thunderstorm. She didn't want to be caught outdoors when it arrived.

What she did instead was go into the dining room with her pistols and gun-cleaning kit. She disassembled her Glock and her snub-nosed .38, carefully cleaned and oiled them, and reassembled them. She loaded both guns and holstered them, one on her hip, the other on her ankle. Then, as an afterthought, she made sure her Swiss Army knife was in her hip pocket. Not that it made any sort of useful weapon, but you never knew. Maybe she should invest in a bigger, nastier knife, like Vic and Corky carried.

It was all paranoia, of course, but she went through the motions anyway. The time was half-past six. She had plenty of morning in front of her, so she decided to go downstairs for a real breakfast and let Carlyle sleep. Rolf was eager to accompany her. He was watching her anxiously, picking up on her mood, but he was only worried because she was. If she could calm down, he'd cheer right up. She scratched him behind the ears and felt a little better. Then they went down to the Barley Corner's public room.

"Oh my God," Erin said when she opened the door.

The room was littered with bodies. Irishmen were slumped on tables, in booths, on the floor. She saw one man spread-eagled on the bar. There must have been fifteen limp forms, scattered every which-way.

After the first initial shock, Erin's brain started working again. She saw no blood. Her horror turned to suspicion, which was confirmed when she distinctly heard a snore from one of the bodies.

This was no massacre. It was just the aftermath of the all-night party. Erin walked into the room, rolling her eyes. A pair of the clean-cut young men she'd noticed the previous night stirred. They were near the door and appeared to be wide awake, alert, and sober.

"Ma'am," one of them said, nodding politely to her.

"You work with Ian?" she asked him.

"Yes, ma'am."

"Serve with him?"

"First tour, ma'am. In the sandbox. Few years back." He meant he'd been in Iraq.

"Marine Corps?" she guessed.

He smiled slightly. "Semper fi, ma'am." Like Ian, he had a very short haircut, a few visible tattoos, a couple of scars, and a calm, confident manner. He was wearing an open button-down shirt over an undershirt, and Erin would bet he had a handgun tucked into the back of his belt.

"Well, keep up the good work," she said. "Have you heard from Ian?"

"Not since last night, ma'am. He's out on an op."

"I know," she said. "I was just wondering if he'd checked in."

"Negative."

She nodded and went to the bar. Danny worked the late shift and she didn't know this other guy, Matt, as well. But he was a nice enough guy.

"Get you something, Ms. O'Reilly?" he asked.

"Bacon and eggs, scrambled, and a cup of coffee," she said. While he went back to the kitchen, she looked curiously around the room. Sure enough, she saw a shock of red, curly hair sticking out of one of the back booths. She walked over and found the hair attached to Corky's head. Rolf sniffed the Irishman and glanced at Erin. The K-9's tail waved noncommittally.

"Passed-out drunk," Erin said in disgust. "Too much punch."

"What's that?" Corky muttered without opening his eyes. "Who's there?"

"It's the ghost of a past girlfriend," she said. "I heard you were seeing a new girl and I'm jealous."

"Of Shelley? What for?"

Erin felt a sudden spike of alarm. "What did you say?" she asked sharply.

Corky opened his eyes and stared blearily at her. "Oh, Erin? It's you, love. I fear I'm not myself this morning. I don't suppose I could trouble you for a glass of beer with a raw egg in it? Sure cure for a hangover."

She bent over him, bringing her face within six inches. The smell of stale beer slapped her in the face like a damp shower curtain but she ignored it. "Your new girl, Corky. The one you've been seeing. What's her name?"

He was fully awake now, in spite of the hangover. "I don't see that's any of your business, love," he said, trying to scoot away from her on the bench. "You gave up any claim to me when—"

She planted a hand just above his shoulder on the bench, leaning even closer and trapping him in place. "Who is she?" she demanded.

He winced at her raised voice and smiled weakly. "A bit quieter, if you please, love. Your voice may be musical, but right now it's like bloody great cymbals in my ears."

Nobody had ever accused Erin of having a musical voice. She was a tone-deaf girl from Long Island. But she knew Corky and she knew he was just trying to change the subject. "Give me a goddamn name," she growled.

"Shelley's a common enough name," he said. "I believe it's short for Michelle."

Erin grabbed the collar of his shirt in her free hand. She twisted the fabric, drawing it tight around his throat.

"That's my sister, Corky!" It came out as a snarl.

"Sister-in-law," he corrected, as if that made it any better.

"She's married to my brother! God damn it! What were you thinking?"

"She came to me," Corky retorted. He tried to pull loose, but Erin held on tight.

"Everything okay, ma'am?" one of the guards asked. He was standing about ten feet off, looking concerned.

"Not your problem. Stay out of this." She turned her attention back to Corky. "What are you talking about?"

"Let go of my bloody neck and give me a chance to explain," he said. "If you want answers, you'd best stop choking the lad who's talking."

Erin reluctantly loosened her grip. Corky sat up and straightened his collar.

"Talk," she said grimly. She stayed standing, leaning her hands on the table and glaring at him.

"I saw her a few days ago," he explained. "You know the lass stands out. I'm surely going to notice a colleen with a face and figure like hers, though how she's held onto it after popping out a pair of bairns I'm sure I don't know."

"You really want to bring the kids into this?" she asked warningly.

"She was looking for a good time, a lad to appreciate her. What was I supposed to say?"

"You were supposed to say no!" Erin snapped. "Damn it, didn't you know who she was?"

He shrugged. "What was the harm, love? Sometimes something like this is just the sort of spice a lass needs to bring some spark back into her marriage. I was just giving her what she wanted."

Erin grabbed him by the collar again and shook him. "Don't you dare," she said. "You don't get to play the good guy here. This is my family you're talking about! I ought to kick your ass!"

"When she got cold feet, I backed off," Corky protested. "I didn't hurt her, hardly touched her. Nothing happened!"

"Plenty happened," she said. "You think it only matters if you screwed her? Yeah, that's how men think, I guess. Shit! Did you even think how much damage you've caused?"

"For the last time, Erin, it wasn't me," he said, pulling loose again. Now he looked angry. "You think I asked dear Shelley to come down to this pub and throw herself at the first likely lad who tossed a smile her way? How much better you think she'd have fared with one of those big Teamsters, once he's got a few beers in him? If you're angry at anyone, be angry with her. I'm not promised to another."

"Oh, I've got plenty of anger to go around," she said. "Damn you, Corky, she wasn't supposed to be part of this."

"And you just thought you could keep your family separate while you're living with one of us?" Corky shot back. "How's that been working out for you?"

Erin almost strangled on her indignation. A thousand angry words tried to squeeze out of her throat at once. What came out was, "Shelley's a good woman. She believes the best in people. But that's because she doesn't know you. You're a goddamned disgrace. I'd tell you to be ashamed of yourself, but it'd be a waste of breath. You don't know the meaning of the fucking word. Go to hell."

Forgetting completely about her breakfast, just needing to get out of there, she turned on her heel and stormed out of the pub. Rolf, mystified but obedient, trotted at her heels.

"Ma'am," the guard said. "Just a second."

"What the hell do you want?" she snapped, spinning to confront him.

"No disrespect, ma'am," he said. "Mr. Carlyle just said to make sure you got to your car okay, when you left. I'll just walk with you, tag along for a minute, okay?"

"Suit yourself," she said. Then, not caring whether he followed her or not, she left the Corner and crossed the street to the parking garage. Her Charger sat in its proper place, a black, unmarked police vehicle with an aggressive front profile and eight cylinders under the hood. Its grille looked like it was growling.

She was angry and confused, but not entirely careless. She was still thinking about car bombs, so she had Rolf check out the wheel wells ad undercarriage. He found no explosives, so she got in and started the engine. Her escort stepped out of the way and watched her pull out of the garage.

It was only a few minutes to the Precinct 8 station, not nearly long enough to decompress. Erin was still fuming when she got there..

Chapter 7

Nobody else was in Major Crimes when Erin arrived. That wasn't surprising; she was an hour early. While Rolf sat in his usual spot beside her desk, she went into the break room and started the coffee machine with quick, savage movements.

Corky! What was he thinking? What was Michelle thinking? That man was nothing but trouble wearing a smile and an Irish accent. Erin had thought she'd been as upset about her sister-in-law as she could be, but knowing who the man was only made it worse. She could just see the two of them, hear Corky sweet-talking Michelle and poor, romantic, silly, foolish Shelley soaking it all up.

Erin realized she was gripping the Formica countertop so hard her fingers were trembling. She made herself take a breath and let go. She went back to her desk to wait for the coffee to brew up.

She should have hit him, should have just hauled off and punched him right in his grinning, sexy, troublemaker's face. Why hadn't she? Because he hadn't been fighting back. Erin was a fighter, not a thug or a bully. She had trouble hitting a man who couldn't, or wouldn't, fight back. And Corky would never hit her. It gave him an infuriating invulnerability.

"Morning, Erin."

She almost jumped out of her shoes, shoving back from her desk and scrambling to her feet. Heart pounding, she looked wildly toward the stairwell. Skip Taylor looked back with a baffled smile. The bomb tech was holding a manila folder in one hand, the other raised in a hesitant greeting.

"What the hell, Skip?" she gasped, trying to recover. "Didn't hear you come up."

"Relax," he said. "Maybe you need to go a little easier on the coffee. That stuff'll wreck your heart."

"Yeah, right," she said. "And Lieutenant Webb will give up smoking and Vic will pour his vodka down the drain. Coffee's not even ready yet. What're you doing up here?"

He smothered a yawn. "I've been working on your car bomb."

"All night?"

"Roger that. Just finished my inspection. I'll want to keep at it, but I figured you were on a clock here and you'd want what I had."

"You figured right. C'mon over and show me what you've got."

"You okay, Erin?"

"Why wouldn't I be?"

He gave her a look, but decided not to press the issue. He walked over to her desk, opened the folder, and spread out a series of photographs of bomb debris.

"Okay," he said. "First things first. It's an ANFO bomb, just like we figured. It's a kitchen job."

"Meaning what?"

"Homemade. Like, out of stuff you'd find in the kitchen. No military components. No C4, no Primacord, none of that fancy stuff. The only thing that's not over-the-counter is the booster."

"Skip, I took a three-week course in demolitions four years ago," she said. "I'm having a lousy morning, and I still haven't had my coffee. Translate, please."

"ANFO is a tertiary explosive," Skip explained. "It's pretty stable. You can't set it off with just a detonator. You need something with a little more bang. That's the booster. Remember that bomb in the parking garage last year?"

"Yeah." Erin wasn't likely to forget that particular incident. She'd only barely survived.

"That was ANFO boosted with C4. Based on chemical residue, it looks to me like this was boosted with plain old dynamite. The type you'd use in construction or mining."

"Common and hard to trace," she said gloomily.

"Exactly," he said. "But we can still figure out some things. Our boy didn't use commercial ANFO. He mixed it himself."

"How can you tell?"

"He used too much fuel oil."

"So he's an amateur?"

Skip shook his head. "No. He knows his stuff. If you're mixing this at home, it's better to have too much oil than too little. Too little and the reaction is weakened. Too much and it still blows up fine, you just get more oil fumes afterward. And I'm pretty sure he just used one stick of dynamite. Our boy was pretty efficient with the expensive part of his bomb."

"So he's a professional," she tried. She was just guessing now and both of them knew it.

"I think so. Or at least the guy who built the bomb is. No way to know if that's the same one who planted it. Here's the thing, Erin. This bomb was built for a specific purpose."

"Yeah, to kill Mickey Connor."

Skip shook his head again. "I don't think so. This bomb was built to be spectacular. To make a statement."

"A car bomb's a pretty damn big statement no matter what," she said.

"True. But you want to think who you're making the statement to. Maybe it was supposed to say to this Connor punk, 'Hey look, asshole, we could've blown you clean into the East River from here.' Like, some sort of warning."

Erin hadn't considered that. "Hold on. You think this whole thing was just street theater?"

He shrugged. "Nobody died, and this was one big damn bomb. Erin, I've been looking at that Hummer for hours. That thing's a goddamn tank. If I wanted to take it out, I would've forgotten about homemade bombs and used a freaking missile launcher. The plates in the door panels would stop a fifty-caliber round. You could go nuts on it with a machine-gun and the guy inside wouldn't care. Either our bomber didn't have the slightest idea what Connor was driving around, or he had no intention of killing him. How much does Connor know about bombs?"

"Bombs?" she echoed. "I have no idea. He's a mob enforcer, so I guess he knows some basics, but he's a former prizefighter, not a soldier. I don't think he's got any formal training."

"Hmm," Skip mused. "So he might not know what was going on. He'd just assume it was a botched hit."

"Bottom line, Skip," she said. "What's your opinion?"

"Well, I'm not a detective," he said, winking. "But if I were, I'd say somebody planted this little party favor with the intention of scaring the hell out of his target. That's a little weird, because it's a lot of trouble to go to just to make a statement like that."

"Or maybe they wanted Mickey to think they were trying to kill him," she said. "But that's insane. Mickey's a violent psychopath. He doesn't scare easy. You hit him, he just hits you back harder."

"Then the bomber better hope your guy doesn't know it was him," Skip said. "Or he's going to have a really bad day. Oh, a couple other things. It looks like the device was planted inside the car, under the hood next to the engine block, and it was wired to the ignition. So it was only going to go off when someone started the car. That nightclub didn't look like it had valet parking."

"No," she said absently.

"Good luck for the valets," he said. "But it was on the wrong side of the engine block, too. That actually shielded the driver from most of the blast. It's possible that even without the armor, he might've lived through it."

"So your conclusion is that this is either the most incompetently placed car bomb you've ever seen, or it was placed by a very competent guy who didn't want to kill Mickey, or even badly hurt him."

"That's about it," he said. "I hope it helps. Oh, and this probably isn't a Carlyle Special."

Erin gave him a swift, searching look. Skip knew Carlyle's history as a bomb-maker for the IRA and had studied his handiwork. Erin was already sure Carlyle hadn't made the bomb, but it was reassuring to hear Skip confirm it.

"Why do you think that?" she asked, just to hear what he'd say.

"It's just a little sloppy. Cars Carlyle's work is very tidy, very professional. He would've gotten the fuel-oil mix perfect. And he doesn't like dynamite. He prefers to work with military-grade explosives. More stable, more predictable."

"Have you studied all his bombs?"

"All the ones we know are his, plus the bombs from the Garbage War in the late '90s," he said, referring to the struggle between the Mafia and the O'Malleys over control of the Long Island garbage-collection rackets. "Those were probably him, though we never proved it. But I've seen all his files from Northern Ireland. I know his style and this isn't it."

"I guess there's a downside to being an artist," she said dryly.

"He might as well sign his name when he plants one," Skip agreed. "Anyway, here's the file. I'll be downstairs, putting pieces of the car back together. Maybe I'll find something else that'll catch your guy for you. Sorry, no fingerprints or anything. The bomb casing was cardboard, if you can believe it, and it pretty much disintegrated with the blast. No shrapnel. Just another indication our boy wasn't looking for body count. Random bystanders ought to thank him."

"I'm thanking you," she said. "Good work, Skip. And sorry I snapped at you."

He grinned. "Sure thing. Just remember, if you ever see me running..."

"I'll try to catch up," she said, finishing the old Bomb Squad joke.

*   *   *

Finally fortified with a cup of coffee, Erin started looking over the files of criminals known to use car bombs. But she kept thinking about her upcoming meeting with Evan O'Malley and Mickey Connor. And, of course, there was the whole mess with Corky and Michelle. She couldn't keep her mind on the case.

Regardless, the meeting with Mickey was probably the most important thing she'd do. Not only was it literally a matter of life and death, but it gave her a chance to dig up more dirt on the O'Malleys. That reminded her of what she needed to do. She had a phone call to make.

Out of an excess of paranoia, she left the station and took Rolf down to the end of the block. She used her special burner cell to place the call.

Her contact picked up on the second ring. "Can you talk?" he asked.

"Yeah, everything's fine," she said.

"Good," Phil Stachowski said. "Is this about the bombing?"

"Yeah. Things are escalating. Mickey went after one of Carlyle's guys last night, put him in the hospital. We've got a meeting with Evan and Mickey at noon, to straighten things out. You got a little time before that?"

"I'll make time. Where do you need me?"

"The meeting's at First Republic Bank, on Sixth Avenue. You know any good restaurants near there?"

"How about Casa Barilla? West 52nd. I can be there at eleven."

"Sounds good. Thanks."

Vic was in the office when she got back, looking like he'd rather be anywhere else. His cheek was pressed against his left fist and his eyes were only half open. The 24-ounce bottle of Mountain Dew in front of him didn't seem to be helping.

"Hey, Vic," she said.

"Huh? What?"

"Nothing. Just making sure you're not dead. What happened to you?"

"Zofia."

Erin raised her eyebrows. "Really?"

"Yeah, really. I hit the Final Countdown with SNEU at the end of their shift. She was still jazzed from the bust."

"So you haven't had any sleep?"

He smiled wryly. "You kidding? We didn't even get out of the bar. That girl dragged me into the bathroom."

"Too much detail, Vic."

"You wanna see the bruises?"

"What part of 'too much' did you not understand?"

"How about you, O'Reilly? You get any last night?"

She made a face. "None of your business."

"So you've been awake all night, too?"

"No! I thought you were talking about sex!"

"Oh. I was talking about sleep."

"Oh."

They looked at each other for a few seconds. Then Vic laughed.

"Seriously, though, Erin. You don't look so good either. Something else happen?"

"No." She could see him noticing her hesitation. "Well, yeah. But it's personal. Not business."

"The Godfather would be so disappointed. What's the problem? Your boyfriend screwing around?"

She shook her head. "No, it's family bullshit. I'm worried about one of my brothers."

"Oh, God." Vic rolled his eyes. "This is what you were talking about yesterday. Like we don't have enough problems with all the heavily armed assholes going around killing each other. He cheating on his wife?"

"No!"

"She cheating on him?"

"Vic!"

He smiled triumphantly. "I thought so! She screwing anybody you know?"

Vic's shrewd guesses were more than a little disconcerting, especially given his fatigue. It was scary to think what he might come up with once he was fully rested. Erin decided the best thing to do was to change the subject completely.

"You want to play detective? How about taking a look at Skip's report? I already went through it. Here it is."

Vic grabbed the file and scanned it for several minutes. When he was done, he set it back on Erin's desk and rubbed his eyes.

"Seems to me like if you want to *not* kill somebody, it's a lot easier to just not plant a bomb in the first place," he said. "Or how about a firecracker? It'd scare the hell out of him just the same, without any of the fuss."

Erin had been thinking about that. "No," she said. "Mickey wasn't supposed to die, but he was supposed to *think* they were trying to kill him. I'm pretty sure this is a false flag operation."

"A frame-up?"

"Yeah. I know a bit about the internal politics of the O'Malleys."

"Do tell," Vic said, deadpan.

She ignored the interruption. "There's three main factions: Evan O'Malley and his loyalists; Mickey Connor, Veronica Blackburn, and their people; and Carlyle, James Corcoran, and their guys. Evan's in charge, but he's been head of the family for decades now, and some of the younger guys are getting impatient. Carlyle is second in command, sort of."

"What do you mean, sort of?"

"He doesn't handle executive action."

"Meaning he doesn't have people killed," Vic said.

"Yeah. He's not on the muscle end. He's more like Tom Hagen in *The Godfather*."

"The *consiglieri*," Vic said. "Knows the business, gives good advice, but doesn't get his own hands dirty. Got it."

"That puts Carlyle in a delicate position," she went on. "If something happened to Evan, Carlyle would be next in line to take over, but he may not have the strength to back up his authority."

"And Connor does," Vic said. "So if the boss goes down, there's a power struggle."

"Exactly. Mickey's got the raw power, but Carlyle has some tough guys he can call on, too. If it comes to a fight between them, maybe everybody loses. Regardless, a bunch of guys get killed."

"How do Connor and Carlyle feel about each other?" he asked.

"They hate each other. Corky and Mickey are even worse. Take away the adult supervision and they'd probably kill each other on sight."

"I've seen those two," Vic said. "Corcoran's a string bean and Connor's a truck. Wouldn't be much of a fight."

"You've never seen Corky move like he means it," she said. "He's *fast*. He's a lot more dangerous than he looks."

"Put two guys in a fight, the big one wins," Vic said with a shrug. "So what's your point?"

"My point is that a struggle between Mickey and Carlyle would be a disaster for the O'Malleys," she said. "So if we're looking for a motive, I think we should be looking at who stands to gain if Evan's boys are at one another's throats."

"Vinnie Moreno?" Vic guessed.

"My thoughts exactly," Erin said.

"But you said he told you he didn't do it," he reminded her.

"No, he said if he wanted Mickey dead, Mickey would be dead. But the point wasn't to kill Mickey."

"That diabolical bastard," Vic said in tones of reluctant admiration. "How do we prove it?"

She threw up her hands. "I have no idea. I guarantee he didn't set the bomb himself. He had to be using somebody else, somebody with access to Mickey's vehicle and knowledge of his movements."

"You think the Lucarellis have a mole in the O'Malleys," Vic said.

"It's the only thing that makes sense," she said.

"Okay. How much of this do you want to put up on the board?" he asked, pointing to the whiteboard.

"None of it."

"Because it's all speculation? What Webb would call thin?"

"Because I don't want any of it getting back to the O'Malleys or the Lucarellis."

"Come on, Erin. Vinnie doesn't have a source in Major Crimes."

She looked at him and said nothing.

"Seriously?" Vic said. "There's three of us in this office. I'm not in bed with the Italians. Webb? Don't make me laugh. And you're in bed with the Irish—literally—but I can't see you working with the Oil Man."

"That was a cheap shot, Vic."

"When that's the shot I've got, I'm taking it," he said.

"Anybody can just walk in here," she said. "I don't trust everyone in this building."

"Yeah? Name one person you don't trust who wears a shield."

"I can't."

"What the hell does that mean?"

Erin raised her eyes toward the ceiling, gesturing with her head toward the upper floors of the building. Specifically, the Internal Affairs office. Vic followed her gaze. His eyebrows quirked together.

"You're kidding," he said quietly.

She shook her head.

He cleared his throat. "Okay. Name another."

"Does it matter, Vic? Let's just leave it off the board for right now. We can always add it later."

"Okay, fine. Have it your way. What's our next move?"

"I'm meeting a couple guys at noon. I may be able to shake something loose."

"Yeah? Who?"

She gave it to him straight. "Evan O'Malley and Mickey Connor. Carlyle's going to be there too."

He whistled. "Okay. I'll be your backup."

"No. No backup."

"The hell with that, Erin. You just told me you're meeting a bunch of Mob guys when there's basically a war going on."

"That's why you can't be there, Vic," she said patiently. "It's okay. I know what I'm doing."

"That's so very comforting."

"You want comfort, go buy yourself a teddy bear."

"You know, I had one of those when I was a kid. You remember those talking teddy bears, with the moving eyes and mouth? The Teddy Ruxpins?"

"Yeah, I think so," she said.

"The sound system on mine went bad and slowed way down," he said. "His voice came out really low, slow, and distorted, like something out of a hole in the ground. *I love you...* Gave me the shivers."

"What'd you do with it?"

"Took it to a vacant lot, doused it with gas, and set it on fire. I figured the goddamn thing was possessed or something. But that freaky bear started talking while it burned. I had nightmares for a month."

"Thank you, Vic, for that heartwarming anecdote from your childhood. Was there a moral to that story?"

"Yeah. The moral is, when the shit goes down, you bring gasoline and matches. Say the word and I'll help you burn these bastards to the ground."

"Thanks, Vic. But today it's just talk. Evan's trying to cool things down between Mickey and Carlyle."

"You don't think Evan did this himself, do you?" Vic suggested. "Maybe he's worried about Carlyle taking over for him, so he's setting Mickey up to kill him."

"Seems a little complicated," Erin said. "Especially considering he could just tell Mickey to kill Carlyle and that's what he'd do."

"Good point. And how sure are you that's not going to happen at this meeting?"

"He wouldn't want a detective present at a murder."

"Sounds like a trap, that's all I'm saying."

"I know what you're saying, Vic. With this sort of thing, I have to go with my gut."

"It's a great day when we trust your life to your small intestine. Where's the meeting?"

"First Republic Bank on Sixth, in the boardroom."

"Ooh, swanky. Comfy leather swivel chairs?"

"I don't know, Vic. I've never been there before."

"See if you can boost one of the chairs for me. I always wanted one of those."

"How would you explain that to the Lieutenant?"

"I'd just say it was all your idea."

Chapter 8

"That's a pretty bare board," Webb observed, staring at the whiteboard. He'd arrived a little after nine. He had his hands wrapped around a fresh cup of coffee and a frown on his face.

"We're still putting things together," Erin said.

"No primary suspect," Webb said. "No motive. No definite answer on where the bomb ingredients were obtained."

"We know what it was," Erin said. "Skip's got a pretty good idea about the bomb composition."

"This isn't chemistry class, O'Reilly. That only helps if it gets us a buyer."

"No good," Vic said. "You can get fertilizer and fuel oil anywhere."

"How about the dynamite?" Webb asked.

"Skip's put a request in to the ATF," Erin said. That was in his report.

"How long will that take?" Webb asked in a tone suggesting he had a pretty good guess.

"Six to eight weeks," she said.

"And it'll just tell us it was construction-grade dynamite like you'd find at any blasting site in America," he said glumly.

"It was stolen, likely as not. So tell me, what do we have that means anything?"

"I'm talking to Mickey Connor again at noon," Erin said. "Evan O'Malley's going to be there, too. I might be able to nail down a motive, find out who's out to get him." She paused. "Vic and I think someone's trying to destabilize the O'Malleys. It's nothing definite, but we think—"

"You think someone's trying to set them against each other," Webb interrupted. "Yeah, I thought of that, too. It's a time-honored way to start a war. It's a good idea to keep your finger on the gang's pulse, O'Reilly. That may help us head off any bloodshed before things go too far. Just be careful at this meeting."

"It's at a Midtown bank," she said. "They wouldn't set it there if they were planning any violence. Between the police and the bank's own security, it's as safe as anywhere in the city."

"Hmm," Webb said noncommittally. "What other irons have we got in the fire?"

"We suspect the Oil Man," Vic said. "I can keep talking to our Narcotics folks and try to put eyes on the Lucarellis. If they're behind this, they'll be looking to capitalize on the confusion. They may start making moves on the street."

"Worth a shot," Webb said. "It could be any other competing gang, too. I want to cross-check known associates of the O'Malleys' rivals for anyone with bomb-making experience."

So Erin spent the next hour and a half looking up the records of every mobster who'd ever blown anything up in New York City. The list was shorter than she might have guessed. Most gangsters preferred guns or knives to explosives. They were easier to use, attracted less official attention, and were less likely to kill the user. Bombings had been more popular in Erin's dad's time with the NYPD. After 9/11, the risk of being labeled a terrorist and getting Homeland Security on your case was much higher and bombs had fallen out of favor.

She thought of calling her dad and asking him, but decided against it. None of the bombers Sean O'Reilly would have known about were still actively blowing things up. Besides, she shied away from talking to any of her family at the moment.

About half past ten, she shut down her computer and stood up. Rolf bounced to his paws and stood at attention.

"I'm going to grab some food and get to my meeting," she announced.

"Don't get murdered by mobsters," Vic said.

"Get us something we can use," Webb said. "Because anything would be better than what we've got."

* * *

Casa Barilla was an informal Italian café, a pleasant place furnished in light-colored wood. Erin was a little early for the lunchtime rush and the place wasn't too crowded yet. She saw Phil Stachowski at once, sitting on a long bench against the right-hand wall. That left Erin a chair opposite him, with her back to the rest of the room. She didn't like it, but somebody had to sit there. Besides, no one was following her. She knew because she'd checked, taking an extra circle around the block to make sure.

"Morning," Phil said. "I've already ordered. I figured everybody likes pepperoni pizza except vegetarians. And I'd bet you aren't one."

"Safe bet," she said, taking a seat.

"How are you holding up?" he asked.

She put out a hand, palm down, and waggled it back and forth in a seesaw motion. "I don't know," she said. "I'm about to talk to a couple of certifiable psychos and try to convince them my boyfriend isn't plotting to murder them. I guess I'm a little tense."

Phil smiled. He was a mild, inoffensive man, bespectacled, balding, and slightly overweight. He was nobody's idea of a hardcore undercover cop, which was exactly the point. No one would ever suspect Phil of being crafty or sneaky. But Lieutenant Stachowski was one of the NYPD's best when it came to handling tough undercover assignments. He'd never lost an officer on an operation. And Erin felt a genuine warmth from him, a sense of confidence and caring. He elicited trust.

"You're doing great, Erin," he said. "Everything set up and working right?"

She nodded. He meant her recording device, sewn into her underwire. That was an advantage to being a female undercover she'd bet they didn't talk about in training. Men didn't have a handy metal framework in their underclothes that could be repurposed. She'd heard J. Edgar Hoover had been in the habit of wearing women's undergarments. Maybe that was why, so he could try out the FBI's listening devices in meetings. Now *there* was a thought.

"Want to let me in on the joke?" he asked, seeing the look on her face.

"Forget about it," she said and stopped smiling. "I just thought we should talk before I go in to see Mickey and Evan."

"Will Carlyle be there, too?"

"Yeah, he's meeting me at the bank just before noon." She'd told him she had a prior commitment, so he was making his own way.

"Does it smell like an ambush?" he asked.

"I don't think so. The meet was Evan's idea, not Mickey's, and Evan's got no reason to go for Carlyle and me. I think he's scared."

"Evan O'Malley is scared?" Phil echoed, raising an eyebrow.

"He'd be nuts not to be," she said. "Mickey's hard to control at the best of times. If Connor really thinks Carlyle tried to kill him, he'll go berserk."

"Erin, this is important." He leaned forward and lowered his voice. "Is Evan in control? Will Connor follow his orders?"

"I hope so," she said. "I think I'll know better after this face-to-face."

"If Evan gets clipped, we're bringing you two in and shutting things down," Phil said. "It'll be way too dangerous. We'll take what we can get. It's not worth your lives."

"We're going to finish the job," she said. "Otherwise we'll never be safe. Think long-term."

"Survival is as long-term as it gets," he said. "You have to be prepared for sudden action here, Erin. Do you have a plan to get you and Carlyle out if things go sideways?"

"We've got cops on practically every street corner," she said. "It's not like we're in the middle of nowhere. What's the matter, Phil? Do you have the heebie-jeebies now?"

"Maybe a little," he confessed. "If you do this long enough, you develop a sensitive internal radar. I've got a feeling about this one. I don't know anything, it's just a hunch. Pay attention to whoever's standing behind you at this meeting."

* * *

The pepperoni pizza hadn't been a good idea, Erin decided. Her stomach was already churning, even without the added irritation of spicy Italian food. She wondered what was in pepperoni, then wondered why she'd never wondered before. Then she decided she'd rather not know. She walked into the bank, went up to one of the tellers, identified herself, flashed her shield, and explained she was there for a scheduled meeting.

The nice thing was that as a police officer, she could openly carry a gun and lead her K-9 even into places with metal detectors that didn't allow pets. Whatever goons Evan showed up with would have to leave their firepower outside. As she was thinking this, a manager bustled over and led her to an elevator.

The doors slid shut and the car hummed upward. Erin heard Ian's voice in her head, explaining that an elevator was a ready-made kill-box. That was why he never lived above the third floor, so he wouldn't have to ride the things. She'd seen at least one movie where a main character got abruptly blown away in an elevator. Her fingers twitched toward her Glock. She forced her hand to remain still.

The elevator reached its destination and the doors opened on an ordinary empty hallway. No gunmen waited to shoot her. Erin felt silly.

"Just on your left, here," the manager said, opening the door for her. "Eileen will be right outside if you need anything. Just let her know."

Eileen, a perky brunette, gave Erin a dazzling smile that could've been used in a toothpaste commercial. Erin never completely trusted anyone with teeth that perfect.

The meeting room had a long conference table of gleaming wood surrounded by black leather chairs. They did indeed look very comfortable, but Erin couldn't think how she'd be able to smuggle one back to the Eightball for Vic. On one side of the table sat Carlyle, already getting to his feet to welcome her. At the far end was Evan O'Malley, fingers steepled in front of him, staring thoughtfully ahead. Carlyle had one of Ian's buddies standing against the wall at his back. The bodyguard was at parade rest, feet spread, hands clasped behind his back. Evan had brought two of his own goons, one on each side. Erin just had Rolf, but in a room where she wore the only guns, she and the K-9 needed no backup.

"Miss O'Reilly," Evan said, and now he did stand up and extend a hand. "Thank you for coming on such short notice." His voice was cold but polite. His fingers were slightly cool to the touch, his grip firm.

"Glad to be here," she said. "Where's Mickey?"

"On his way," Evan said.

"We've some refreshments," Carlyle said, pointing to a tray which held a coffeepot and some cookies.

"I just had lunch," she said, thinking if she put one more thing in her stomach, she'd probably just throw it right back up. Mickey was like a wild jungle animal. He was scary, but if you knew he was out there, you preferred to have him where you could see him.

She circled the table and took the chair just to Carlyle's right. From that position she could cover the door. She realized it would be rude, by mob standards, to have her hand under the table where her gun was, so she forced herself to lay her hands on the tabletop.

"I heard you've got a man in the hospital," Evan said to Carlyle.

"Aye, but he's mending well," Carlyle said.

"Does he need anything?"

"I'm handling it."

Erin checked the clock on the wall. It read 11:57.

"You sure Mickey's coming?" she asked Evan.

"He said he'd be here," Evan said. That was clearly good enough for him. Nobody stood Evan O'Malley up.

"We've a couple minutes yet," Carlyle said. "I trust Mr. Connor's not seriously injured?"

"No," Evan said.

Rolf, uninterested in the human small talk, was sniffing around under the conference table. He was particularly interested in the hollow column that supported the end of the table nearest Evan. If it'd been a fire hydrant, Erin would've expected him to cock a leg on it.

"Mr. O'Malley," Erin said. "Have you considered the possibility that this bomb wasn't intended to kill Mickey?"

"It was a very large explosive device," Evan pointed out.

"It was placed in the wrong part of the car," she said. She was getting edgier, more impatient and anxious by the moment. "But we should be talking to Mickey about this. He should be here by now. Where the hell is he?"

Carlyle laid a hand on hers. "What are you thinking, darling?" he asked quietly.

"He's planning something," she said. Then a sudden, horrible thought hit her. "Mr. O'Malley, did your people sweep this room?"

"For what?" Evan asked. His voice took on an even harder edge than usual.

Erin ignored him. "Rolf," she said.

The Shepherd paused, one paw raised, head cocked at her.

"*Such!*" she ordered.

Rolf took another sniff at the table. Then he sat facing the table leg, completely still.

"God," Erin whispered. She was a woman of action, but for just a second, she couldn't move.

Carlyle understood. "Out! Now!" he snapped at his boss.

"Everyone!" Erin added, waving her hands and coming to her feet. "Out of the building! Now!"

Erin didn't know if Evan entirely realized what was going on, but the man hadn't gotten to be an old mobster without developing a keen survival instinct. The O'Malley chieftain was up and moving with surprising speed for a man his age.

"You too, lad," Carlyle added to his bodyguard. "Tell the people downstairs. They'll need to evacuate the building."

"We need to go," Erin said. "*Right now.*"

"No time," he said. "Your dog says there's a device. If it's set for noon, we'll never get everyone out in time." He was already down on his back under the table, examining the wood veneer.

Erin knew he was right. There was simply no way to evacuate a multi-floor office building in a couple of minutes. 9/11 had made that painfully clear. Rolf was telling her an explosive was hidden in the table. She had no way of knowing how big it was. If it went off, people would die. Maybe a few, maybe a lot, but she and Carlyle would certainly be among them. The clock now read 11:59.

Carlyle was an expert bomb-maker. If anyone could deactivate it, he was their best bet. There wasn't time to wait for the Bomb Squad.

"What do you need?" she asked, kneeling beside him.

"Screwdriver," he said.

Erin snatched out her Swiss Army knife and fumbled open the screwdriver attachment. She handed it to him.

The Irishman's fingers were a blur, frantically unscrewing a panel. It came off to reveal a bundle of fiber-optic cables that ran up to ports on the tabletop, built so executives could plug in their laptops during meetings.

An earsplitting noise erupted on all sides, a high-pitched, rhythmic, insistent beeping synced to bright flashing lights. Erin jumped, then recovered. Carlyle's guy must have triggered the fire alarm. That was a good idea; Erin wished she'd thought of that herself. It would get everyone moving with no need for an explanation.

"There it is," Carlyle said. He reached into the bundle of cables and started cutting wires loose. "Darling, you ought to be running."

"No time," Erin said. Her mouth felt very dry.

"Then get to the far end of the room and lie down, please." Carlyle was as polite as ever, but his teeth were clenched and his voice showed the tension he was feeling.

"Rolf, *komm*," Erin ordered. She hurried to the end of the room furthest from Carlyle. "*Platz*," she added.

Rolf flattened himself on his belly and put his head between his paws, staring at her with his big brown eyes. Erin lay down and curled herself protectively around her dog, putting a hand over his ears. She opened her mouth, knowing if a bomb went off, it might keep the pressure wave from bursting her eardrums. Not that she expected to survive. The fire alarm continued its monotonous, earsplitting noise.

She closed her eyes and waited, mouthing a silent prayer.

A hand fell on her shoulder. She twitched in surprise. Then she opened her eyes and looked up.

Carlyle stood there, holding something in his hand. It looked like an ordinary length of pipe, about three inches across and a foot long. His tie was askew and lines of sweat stood out on his face, but he was smiling grimly.

"It's safe?" she asked.

"Aye, we're fine," he said. "Pipe bomb. It was wired to a cell phone, but I've cut it loose and detached the detonator. It's plastic explosive, perfectly stable on its own. Simple device, really, no anti-tampering measures. The rest of that column is packed with bags of ball bearings."

Erin winced. That would have created a storm of shrapnel that would have shredded everyone in the room. "Mickey?" she guessed.

He nodded. "It's the only reason the lad wouldn't be present."

"Let's get out of here," she said.

At that moment, an incongruous sound cut through the fire alarm. It was a generic cell-phone ringtone. Erin crouched and looked under the table. She saw a cheap prepaid phone merrily ringing away on the end of a couple of freshly-cut wires.

"Jesus," she murmured. If they'd been thirty seconds slower, that would have been the last sound any of them heard.

"Your knife," Carlyle said, handing it to her. "Thanks for the use of it, darling."

* * *

By the time Erin, Carlyle, and Rolf exited the bank, three police cars were on scene and half a dozen uniforms were trying to take charge of the situation. Bank employees and customers were milling around in confusion. Erin was holding Rolf's leash. Carlyle was still carrying the pipe bomb. Nobody was paying any attention to him. It was a fire alarm, not a bomb scare, so the well-dressed man with the piece of pipe in his hand attracted no notice.

"Where's Evan?" she asked, looking over the scene. She didn't see him anywhere.

"That lad's no fool," Carlyle said. "He's long gone. And we'd best be leaving too."

"I'm a cop, remember?" she told him. "I'm not going to get in trouble. And you just saved more than one life. We'll be fine. We didn't do anything."

Carlyle's bodyguard emerged from wherever he'd been, coming up alongside his boss. "Orders, sir?" he asked quietly.

"Mickey's expecting an explosion," Carlyle said. "We have to assume he's got eyes on this place, whether he's personally present or not. We don't want to be standing here in the open."

"He really tried to take Evan out," Erin said. She hadn't believed he would go for it.

"And you and me into the bargain," he said. "Rolf, too, come to that. But he missed, and now it's Mickey will be running scared. Evan's not one to forget this, nor forgive. But you'll pardon me if I've no wish to be caught between the two of them."

Erin nodded, but something else had caught her attention. The senior Patrol officer on scene, a grizzled old sergeant, was talking into his radio. The man's expression suddenly froze. Then he was waving his arms and shouting to his men.

"We got a 10-13!" he yelled. "Officers down!"

Just like that, the situation was turned on its head. The uniforms didn't know about the bomb; all they knew was that someone had yanked a fire alarm in a Midtown bank. If the bomb had gone off, it would be different. But these cops saw no signs of smoke or fire. For all they knew, it was a prank or a mechanical malfunction. A 10-13, the call "officer in need of assistance," trumped all the ordinary everyday bullshit. And if officers really were down, the entire NYPD had a brand-new top priority.

Erin left Carlyle and his guy standing where they were and sprinted toward the sergeant. She was less than twenty yards away, but by the time she got there, two carloads of cops were already loaded and pulling away from the curb, sirens howling, and the sergeant was getting into his own car.

"O'Reilly, Major Crimes," she barked, holding up her shield. "What's the call?"

"Active shooter," the sergeant said over his shoulder. "West 86th and West End. We got two officers down! I gotta roll!" Then he, too, was gone.

Erin felt like a cold fist had punched straight into her guts, grabbed them, and twisted hard. It wasn't the news that two of her fellow officers were wounded, maybe dead. It was the address. That street corner was less than half a block from her brother's house.

She ran for her car. The Charger was in one of the police spaces near the bank's entrance. She hauled out her keys and popped the locks, yanking the back door open for Rolf. The Shepherd hopped into his compartment, all tail-wagging excitement. He could feel her sudden burst of energy and knew they were going to work. He didn't understand any of the rest of it. This was all a game to him.

She slid behind the wheel and shoved the key into the ignition, giving it a savage twist. The Charger's engine roared to life.

The passenger door opened and a man tumbled in beside her.

"What the—" she began.

"Explain on the way," Carlyle said.

Erin floored the accelerator, leaving patches of rubber on the street. She steered with one hand and activated the flashers and siren with the other. Her seatbelt alarm beeped at her, but she had other things to worry about. She slalomed around cars that were too slow to get out of the way, still driving one-handed, grabbing the car's radio with her off-hand and turning on the police band.

"*Nine Victor Charlie on scene,*" a man she didn't know was saying. "*We need multiple buses forthwith. Two officers down, one nonresponsive. We got other casualties, too. Looks like a gunfight. I see one in the street, a crashed vehicle with at least one more. Get me more units here!*"

"*Copy that, Nine Victor Charlie,*" Dispatch replied. "*All available units are inbound, ETA momentary. Are you taking fire?*"

Erin made a hard turn. The squeal of the brakes was almost drowned out by the shriek of the siren. Her jaw was clenched so tight she could feel her teeth grinding.

"*Negative, Dispatch,*" the first voice said. "*Looks like the shooting's over.*"

"Where are we going, darling?" Carlyle asked.

"Crime scene," she said in a tight, tense voice. She reached for her seatbelt and yanked it across her chest. Then she put both hands on the wheel, and she needed them. She was driving way too fast for Manhattan roads and traffic, in spite of her flashers and siren.

"This has something to do with you?" he guessed.

"These guys were shot right outside Sean and Shelley's front door," she said.

"But surely they'll know better than to get involved in a shootout," he said. "They'll have stayed indoors. I'm certain they're fine."

"Think of the timing!" she snapped, swerving to avoid a double-parked panel truck and making a yellow cab take desperate evasive action. "You think it's a coincidence?"

"What do you need from me?" Carlyle asked in a softer tone.

"I don't know yet," she said, and then they were there.

Erin was lucky to have been in Midtown already, just a couple minutes from the scene. Six squad cars had gotten there ahead of her, and she could hear more sirens converging, but she was in the second wave. She threw the Charger into park and jumped out, leaving Carlyle and Rolf in the car.

Most of the cops were clustered around another Patrol car whose doors stood open. Two men wearing NYPD blue lay on the ground. Uniforms were frantically performing first aid on them. The car was pockmarked with bullet holes and the passenger-side window was a spider-web of cracked safety glass. Further down the street, another body lay on the blacktop in a pool of blood. Erin could also see what looked like some sort of car crash right in front of her brother's brownstone. A black

SUV had plowed into a parked blue mini-Cooper. Steam was rising from the crumpled hood.

Erin was momentarily overwhelmed by the sheer chaos of the scene. Two officers were examining the crashed car. Another was standing over the downed guy in the street. She headed that way first, figuring she couldn't do anything for the wounded cops that wasn't already being done.

The uniform standing over the body wasn't trying to help him. The patrolwoman was pointing her gun at him instead. She had her foot resting on a sleek black automatic pistol she'd just kicked out of the downed man's hand.

"What's going on?" Erin demanded. "O'Reilly, Major Crimes."

"Calloway, from the Two Six," the uniform said. "Crazy son of a bitch was down when I got here, but he still had his gun in his hand. I'm lucky he was empty or he could've shot me."

"Is he dead?" Erin asked, dropping to one knee.

"Careful," Calloway warned, but Erin wasn't listening to her anymore. All she could hear was the roaring of her own blood in her ears. A wave of dizziness washed over her. She thought she might faint, or maybe throw up.

"Oh, no," she murmured. "No, no, no."

The man in the street was lying on his stomach. His skin, sheet-white from shock, was streaked with blood. But his features were ones she would have recognized almost anywhere. Ian Thompson lay in his own blood, head turned to one side, eyes half-open, staring at nothing.

Chapter 9

"Come on, come on," Erin said under her breath, feeling for a pulse.

"Detective, this guy shot two of ours," Calloway said. "Do you really think—"

"Shut up and help me or get the hell out of my way!" Erin snapped. She felt it then: a faint, weak pulse. Relief and fresh fear hit her a vicious one-two emotional punch. "Stay with me, Ian. Stay with me."

She looked wildly around. "Get a paramedic!" she shouted at Calloway. "This guy's one of ours! Grab a first aid kit! Go!" There was no time to explain. If Calloway thought Ian was an undercover cop, Erin didn't care, just as long as it got him the help he needed.

Calloway nodded doubtfully, but the urgency in Erin's voice got her moving back toward the other cops. Erin didn't waste any more time on the Patrol officer, turning her attention back to the wounded man.

"Oh God," Erin muttered under her breath. What had Ian done? What had she made him do? She'd set him off about being a hero, and here he was, shot to pieces practically on her brother's front step. She knew she shouldn't move him, for fear he might have spinal damage. It was tricky to find where he'd been hit. The whole front of his body was soaked in blood. She saw an exit wound high up on the shoulder. Another shot had clipped his neck, narrowly missing his carotid artery. She knew he had to have been hit more, given the sheer volume of blood loss, but couldn't see the holes.

"Corps... corpsman," Ian mumbled. He was shivering, a clear sign of serious shock. In his delirium, he'd flashed back to his time in the military.

"They're on their way, Marine," she said, wondering whether he even knew where he was. "Keep talking. Stay with me. Stay awake."

Ian's left hand was clenched around something. He was making feeble movements with it, trying to lift the hand. Erin saw another bullet had punched into his left bicep, gouging a path through the tattoo on his arm.

She put pressure on two of the wounds she could see, the neck and the shoulder, but she didn't have enough hands. The blood was pumping out in a steady flow, not in arterial spurts. Maybe he'd make it. Or maybe his blood pressure was just too low to force the blood out of him anymore. Where was the damn ambulance?

"Erin?" The voice was Carlyle's, just over her shoulder. "Erin, darling, what... oh mother of God. Ian, lad?"

Carlyle's voice cracked. He slumped to the ground next to Erin, the knees of his fine gray suit sinking into the pool of blood. He didn't care, or even notice. He was staring at the young man he loved like a son. His calm, handsome face had crumbled into a ruin of raw anguish.

"Give me a hand," Erin said. "Pressure here, on his arm. You've always got a handkerchief, right? Tie it around the upper arm, pull it tight. Tight as you can."

Carlyle nodded mutely, taking out his silk pocket handkerchief and doing as Erin told him.

"Ian, buddy. Come on," Erin said. "You're still on the clock, kiddo. You don't get to go home yet. As long as you're breathing, you're still in the fight."

"Sorry," Ian whispered. "Screwed up."

"Forget about it," she said. "You're doing great."

"Connor."

"What?" Erin asked. "What did you say?"

"Connor. Tailed him. Here. Tried to stop him. Took fire." Ian fumbled with the thing in his hand again. His fingers opened a little and Erin saw he was holding a box magazine for an automatic pistol, full of cartridges. "Dropped my gun..."

Erin's eye trailed to the pistol Calloway had been standing on. It was one of Ian's Beretta nine-millimeters. Its slide was locked back. The gun was empty. Ian had been shot, she didn't even know how many times, but he was still trying to reload and finish the fight.

"Lad?" Carlyle said in a shaking half-whisper. "Talk to me, lad."

But Ian didn't answer. His eyes rolled back in his head and he made a choking, coughing sound in his throat.

"Get his airway clear," Erin said. "We need to tilt his head, like this. Careful, he might have spinal damage." She saw the paramedics arriving on scene, but were they too late?

"Here," she told Carlyle, handing him her shield. "Get one of the docs over here right now. Show them this." She turned back to Ian. "Don't worry, kiddo. They're here. We're going to get you fixed up. You'll be just fine."

But another fear was on her, the same one that had made her drive to this damned street in such a rush. What was Mickey doing on this block? He had no reason to be here, none whatsoever. He didn't even know Sean and Michelle O'Reilly.

Except maybe he did. Erin remembered the car that had driven away from her late-night meeting with Michelle. She thought of how Shelley had been coming to the Barley Corner, how she'd taken up with James Corcoran. Mickey could have been there at any time, watching, learning, plotting. If he felt Erin and Carlyle had personally attacked him, he'd retaliate. Evan O'Malley wouldn't hit family members in reprisal for an attack, but Mickey would.

Scarcely aware of what she was doing, Erin stood up. She had tunnel vision, everything around her retreating into a nondescript blur as she looked across the street. The front door of Sean and Michelle's brownstone was standing halfway open.

Carlyle was coming back, running, a paramedic beside him. He dropped down beside Ian again. Tears were streaming down his cheeks. He was saying something, but the words meant nothing to Erin. It was all just so much gibberish. The EMT got down and started to treat Ian.

Erin took a stumbling step toward the brownstone, then another. Then she broke into a run. Someone shouted at her. A Patrol cop put out a hand. She paid no attention. She went up the steps two at a time. The door was a good, solid one made of real hardwood, but the knob and lock-plate were torn clean out of the wood, the screws bent and twisted. Splinters of wood were strewn across the entryway.

Erin pulled her Glock, heart hammering. "Sean!" she cried. It was almost a scream. "Shelley!"

All she heard in answer were the voices of police outside and the infernal chorus of sirens.

"Shelley!" she yelled again, desperately. "Anna! Patrick!"

She cleared the downstairs quickly, recklessly, not wanting but needing to see, needing to know for sure. She saw only ordinary everyday things, her brother's family's life laid out in simple, heartbreaking detail. A little tower of wooden blocks

Patrick liked to play with, half-built on the living room floor. Anna's ballet slippers next to the front door. The *New York Times* neatly folded on the coffee table, next to Sean Junior's favorite chair. No blood, no bodies. Thank God for small mercies.

She ran upstairs. The master bedroom was empty, the bed neatly made. Patrick's room was empty. No sign of the boy. Anna's room was deserted, too. Maybe, Erin thought with sudden, desperate hope, they'd gone out somewhere. Maybe they were at the Bronx Zoo, or Central Park, or... or somewhere, *anywhere* but here. She reached for her phone to call Michelle.

"Auntie Erin?"

The little girl's tentative voice made Erin's heart skip. She dropped to her hands and knees and looked under the bed. There was Anna, lying on the floor, and held in her arms was her little brother Patrick. Their eyes were enormous and very frightened. Patrick was clutching the plush sheep Carlyle had given him, a fluffy talisman.

"Are you hurt?" Erin asked.

Anna shook her head.

"You can come out now," Erin said. "It's okay. The police are here. I'm here. You're safe."

Anna crawled out from under the bed. Patrick came with her, still holding his sheep close.

Erin holstered her gun and drew the kids into her arms, hugging them as tight as she dared. "What happened, kiddo?" she asked Anna.

"I was playing with My Little Ponies. The doorbell rang. I heard something break downstairs and Mommy screamed. Where's Mommy?"

Erin tightened her jaw and tried to keep her voice calm and level. "I don't know, kiddo. But I'm going to try to find her. What happened then?"

"I heard bangs," Anna said. "I think they were gunshots."

"In the house?"

"No, outside. And a man yelled something."

"Did you hear what he said?"

"I think he said, 'Look out, ma'am.'"

Erin swallowed. "Then what?"

"He yelled, 'Get down!' And there was lots more shooting. Like on TV."

"What did you do?"

"I ran and got Patrick. Then I came in here and hid under the bed. They told us in school, if we heard shooting, and there were no grownups around, we should find a place to hide and be quiet until the police came. Where's Mommy?"

"You did exactly the right thing," Erin said. "I'm proud of you, kiddo. You were really brave."

"I want Mommy," Anna said. Her lip quivered. Patrick was crying silently.

How did kids know? Maybe it was something in Erin's own body language. But Anna had always been a bright girl, good at figuring things out. Erin had no idea what to say.

"I need to see what I can find out," she said after a moment. "Maybe I can get some clues that will tell me where your mom is. I want you to stay up here."

Anna and Patrick shook their heads in unison. Both of them were crying now.

"I'll be right downstairs," Erin insisted.

Patrick attached himself to Erin's left leg in a death grip.

Erin sighed. "Okay, you can come with me. But you need to let me work. And you can't touch anything. Nothing, you got it?"

By the time she managed to extricate her leg and get back downstairs, a pair of Patrol officers were standing in the entryway looking tense and a little lost.

"What's going on, Detective?" one of them asked.

"Possible abduction," she said. "Give me your radio."

The other uniform handed her his radio handset. Erin grabbed it.

"Dispatch, this is O'Reilly, shield four-six-four-oh. I need a BOLO on two people. The first is Michelle O'Reilly. Caucasian female, age thirty-nine, five foot ten, weight about one-forty, dark hair, shoulder-length." She paused and glanced at Anna. "Kiddo, what was your mom wearing? This is important. Try to think."

Anna considered. "White," she said. "White shirt with buttons. Where is she?"

Erin went back to the radio. "Ms. O'Reilly was wearing a white button-down blouse when last seen. She's a potential kidnapping victim. Last sighting was the location of the 10-13S."

"Copy that, O'Reilly," Dispatch said. "Second subject?"

"Second subject is Michael Connor, AKA Mickey. Caucasian male, about six-foot-six, weight... shit, I don't know. Call it three hundred. Very muscular. Heavy features, broken nose, facial scars. Blond hair, short haircut, light blue eyes. He's to be considered armed and extremely dangerous, and he's the primary suspect in the shooting of our officers. He may be on foot, or in a vehicle. He'll probably have Ms. O'Reilly with him. If he does, it's an HRT situation." She was referring to the Hostage Rescue Team.

"Copy that," Dispatch said again. "Will advise all officers."

With that done, Erin handed the radio back to the uniform and looked outside. A couple of paramedics had Ian on a stretcher now. One of them was holding a bag over him and was rhythmically squeezing it, forcing air into his lungs. Carlyle was standing next to the gurney, holding Ian's hand. He was bent over the younger man, talking to him.

There was nothing Erin could do for them that the medics couldn't, so she tried to push them out of her mind. She had to think hard, fast, and clearly. Michelle's life might depend on it.

She was aware of fear, clawing its way up from the deep, dark parts of her brain, the parts that remembered the stats regarding kidnapping and victim survival rates. Fear? It was worse than fear; it was blind panic. She couldn't let it out, or she'd lose her shit completely. And she couldn't afford to fall apart now. Too many people needed her.

Anna tugged on her pants leg. "Auntie Erin?"

"Don't worry, kiddo," she said distantly.

"Did Mommy get kidnapped?"

Sometimes Erin wished Anna wasn't such a bright kid. She went to one knee and took the girl's hands in hers, looking her in the eye. Anna's eyes were very large and swimming with tears.

"Anna, I don't know where your mom is. That's what I'm figuring out. But I'm going to do everything I can to find her and bring her back. This is what I do. And you can help me by staying brave."

Anna bit her lip. "I'm scared," she whispered.

"So am I, kiddo. But the thing about being scared is, it gives you the chance to be brave. Can you do that? Can you be a big, brave girl right now? Patrick needs you."

Anna nodded. She took hold of Patrick's hand and held on tight.

"That's my girl," Erin said. "Now, where's your dad?"

"Working."

Erin didn't want to call Sean Junior away from the hospital. Hell, for all she knew, he might be the one they'd need to save one of the wounded cops, or Ian. But she needed someone to take care of the children.

She made her choice. "Come on, kids," she said. "Stay close." She hurried down the front steps and across the street. The medics were getting ready to move Ian and paid no attention. Carlyle looked up. Tears streaked his cheeks. He looked very old in that moment and desperately worried. Then he saw the children tagging along with Erin and his eyes widened.

"I need you," she said to him. "Take care of them."

"Erin," he said and made a helpless gesture toward the stretcher. Ian had a tube in his mouth. His eyes were closed and his skin had a white, waxy look.

"Mickey took Shelley," she said quietly.

She watched Carlyle pull himself together. She'd always known he had a strong will, but seeing him step away from his fear for Ian and refocus himself, through nothing but sheer inner strength, stunned her. He put a gentle smile on his broken face, covering up his pain, and looked down at the O'Reilly kids.

"Your aunt needs to be about her work," he said, and his voice held only the slightest hint of tension. "You'll be staying with me in the meantime. I think we'd best get away from all this noise and confusion. I'm going to take you to my home. Won't that be grand?"

"You know Mr. Carlyle, right, kiddos?" Erin said. "He gave you that sheep, remember?"

Patrick nodded and clutched the fluffy toy closer.

"I'll call my dad," Erin said. "It'll take him a few hours to drive down, but he can take over once he gets here."

"I'll look out for him," Carlyle said. "And don't be worrying about us. I'll hail a cab to take us to the Corner."

"What's his prognosis?" Erin asked one of the medics, pointing to Ian.

"We're just prepping him for transport," the EMT said. "He's taken five bullets and lost a lot of blood. He's critical. He needs surgery, stat."

"You taking him to Bellevue?"

"Yeah."

"Make sure there's a guard," she said. "Major Crimes will need to talk to him."

"Ma'am," the medic said grimly, "I'm just hoping he makes it to the hospital. He won't be talking to anyone anytime soon. Even if he lives."

Erin gritted her teeth, but what could she say? It was in God's hands, and maybe her brother's. She said a quick, silent prayer for the wounded man as the EMTs wheeled Ian to the waiting ambulance. Carlyle was holding Anna's hand. Anna was holding Patrick with her other hand. Patrick still had his sheep.

"Do your job, darling," Carlyle said quietly. "I've got this." He handed her shield back to her, his thumb leaving a perfect, bloody print on the gold metal.

There was so much to talk about, but no time. The crime scene and the trail were getting colder every moment. Erin paused just long enough to give Anna and Patrick each a kiss on the cheek. Then she was running back to her Charger to get Rolf. Maybe his nose could give her the edge she needed.

Chapter 10

On the way back to the O'Reilly house, Rolf's leash in hand, Erin took out her phone with the other. She hit the contact for her parents. This situation called for all hands.

The phone rang once, twice, three times. Then the call went through.

"O'Reilly," said Sean O'Reilly.

"Hey, Dad," she said.

"What's wrong, kiddo?" Sean might be retired, but his police instincts remained razor-sharp, especially when combined with his parental radar.

"Dad, Shelley's been—" she began, then, to her mortification, her voice broke and she had to fight back a sob.

"Didn't copy," he said, lapsing into his old cop lingo. "Repeat?"

She felt a surge of anger at herself. This was no time for weakness. "Shelley's been abducted," she said. "Just a few minutes ago. I'm on scene. The kids are fine. They'll be at my place, with Carlyle. Our apartment above the Barley Corner. Mom's been there, she can tell you where it is. How fast can you get there?"

"I'm on my way," Sean said grimly, all business. "Couple hours, tops. Does Junior know?"

"Not yet. He's at work. We've got a couple ER trauma cases on the way to him right now. I'm going to find her, Dad."

Erin's phone beeped, indicating an incoming call. She looked at the screen and saw Webb's name.

"I have to go."

"Copy that. You got this, kiddo." No more questions, no small talk. Sean O'Reilly was a professional. Erin ended the call and answered Webb.

"O'Reilly."

"Forget about Connor," Webb said. "We've got bigger problems. Two of ours just got shot."

"I know, sir. I'm already there."

"What? How?"

"Heard about it from a couple officers at the bank. Where are you?"

"Neshenko and I are en route. We'll be there in a few minutes. What's that, Neshenko?"

Erin heard Vic in the background. "Got a BOLO, sir. It's for a Michelle... oh shit." Then his voice got too quiet to make out the words.

"I have to go, sir," Erin said, hanging up. The last thing she wanted to do was talk to her commanding officer about her sister-in-law. She was back at the front door now, and it was time to start tracking.

Rolf looked up at her and wagged his tail. He felt the change in her energy. He was ready for whatever she needed.

She tried to think of it like any crime scene, building a map in her head of what had happened. She started with the black SUV in front of the house. A man was slumped over the steering wheel. He'd taken two bullets to the side of the head and was obviously far beyond medical attention, or even the reconstructive skill of a mortician. He'd be getting a closed-casket funeral for sure. Another body was in the back seat on the driver's side. That man was also obviously dead. He'd been hit once at the base of the throat and once just above the bridge of his nose. Either shot would have killed him. He still clutched a pump-action combat shotgun in one hand.

The car itself was pockmarked with bullet holes. Erin counted seven holes in the bodywork: two just below the hood, three in the front door, and two in the back door. The left front tire was also flat, though she couldn't tell if it had taken a hit or been punctured in the collision. It appeared the SUV hadn't been going very fast when it hit the Mini Cooper. The steam was issuing from one of the pistol holes, indicating the radiator had been damaged.

"Damn good shooting," Erin said aloud. She looked back toward the bullet-riddled squad car, then across the street. The way the angles worked out, none of the hits could have come from the cops. Ian had fired every shot that had struck the vehicle.

She went around to the passenger side of the wreck. Both doors on this side stood open. She saw the glint of brass on the sidewalk, like glittering confetti. Quite a few empty cartridge casings were scattered on the ground, suggesting either multiple weapons or a single gun with a high rate of fire. She pulled on a pair of disposable gloves, crouched, and picked up one of the casings. It was for a .45-caliber bullet.

"Submachine-gun," she muttered. She didn't see the gun anywhere, so Mickey had probably taken it with him.

Erin slowly climbed the steps to the O'Reilly front door. She'd rushed in the first time, not bothering to look down. Now she scanned every surface for clues. Rolf, beside her, snuffled at the spent shells.

Several splashes of dark red liquid trailed down the steps.

"Bingo," she said, kneeling and looking closer. It was definitely blood and the trail led down the sidewalk, away from the crashed SUV. She felt a mounting excitement. Maybe Mickey had been wounded. If so, and if he was still on foot, there was a chance to run him down.

Erin pointed to the bloodstains. "Rolf," she said. "*Such!*"

The drops of fresh blood were like brightly lit highway signs for Rolf. He was off and running, nostrils flaring, tail whipping eagerly. Erin jogged behind him, calling to the nearby officers to follow. If Mickey had gone to ground, she didn't want to stumble on him with only the K-9 for backup.

The trail led down the sidewalk in the opposite direction from the shot-up squad car. The wounded man was moving fast, Erin guessed, by the way little droplets had spattered off to either side.

"This the guy who shot our people?" one of the uniforms asked Erin.

"I think so," she said over her shoulder.

"He got tagged, at least," said another cop with angry satisfaction.

"Not hard enough," Erin muttered.

They got to the next street corner. Rolf immediately pulled to the right, around the corner. Erin let him take the lead. He was pulling hard, throwing his shoulders against the leash. His tongue was hanging out. He didn't know what was at stake. For him, it was just another chase, with his rubber Kong ball waiting at the end. But that was plenty for him to put in maximum effort.

The street was pleasant, lined with trees and graceful, beautiful old brownstone houses on either side. Rolf angled toward the curb and pulled into the street. Then he paused. He sniffed the air. His tail wagged more uncertainly. He whined.

"Shit," Erin growled.

"What's up, Detective?" one of the Patrol officers asked, coming up behind.

"He got in a car," she said. "Right here." She kicked the asphalt in frustration. Rolf couldn't track a guy once he got in a sealed vehicle.

"I thought that was the getaway car," the cop said, pointing over his shoulder with a thumb.

"He had another," she said. "Or he stole one."

"Got something here!" the other uniform called. He was peering around the front steps of one of the brownstones.

Erin snatched out her Glock and ran to join him, accompanied by Rolf and the first officer. They saw a man lying in a crumpled heap on the ground. He was wearing a tattered brown jacket and blue jeans. He moved slightly, holding his head.

"NYPD!" Erin snapped. "Keep your hands where I can see them! Sir, can you hear me?"

The man groaned and rolled over onto his back. He was a little guy, about the same height as Erin, olive-skinned and black-haired, sporting a little wisp of a mustache. She guessed he was Middle Eastern, or maybe North African. Arab, at any rate. When he saw the three cops pointing guns at him, he whimpered and held his hands in front of his face.

"Please," he said. "Do not hurt me. I can only pay you a little."

Erin lowered her Glock. If this guy was part of Mickey's crew, she'd eat Rolf's leash, collar and all. "What's your name, sir?" she asked, crouching in front of him.

"Abdul Mohammed Hassan," he said. "Please, madam, I am only a driver. I have twenty American dollars. Here, you take." He started to reach into his pocket.

"Hey! Freeze!" one of the uniforms shouted.

Hassan froze, eyes wide and terrified.

"Cool it, buddy," Erin said to the cop. "And put that gun away. You're scaring the witness. Mr. Hassan, I don't want your money. I'm a detective with the New York Police Department. I'm here to help. What are you doing here?"

"I come to America to work, to find a job," he said.

She sighed inwardly. "No, I mean, what are you doing on this street, today?"

"My job. I drive a taxi. My brother, he owns the company. I drive for him."

"Where's your cab?"

"They took it."

"Who took it?"

"The big man and his friend. He hit me and threw me into the wall."

Erin's heart quickened. "Who was with this big man?"

"Another man, smaller. And a woman."

Erin took out her phone and quickly thumbed through the photo gallery to a picture of Michelle and the kids. She turned the screen toward Hassan. "Was this the woman?"

He nodded. "Yes."

"Was she hurt?"

"I do not know. The other man, the small one, he waved me to stop. When I stopped, I saw the big man was holding the woman by the arm. She looked very frightened. And he was bloody."

"Bloody how? Where was he hurt?"

"Here, I think." Hassan pointed to his own upper arm, just above the elbow. "He was all bloody. When I saw it, I tried to drive away. I wish for no trouble. But the other man stood in front of me and pointed a gun at me. Then the big man pulled on the door. I had locked it. He pulled very hard and broke the handle. Then he was angry and put his hand through the window. The glass broke. He reached in the window and opened the door from inside."

"Damn," one of the cops said quietly, impressed. But Erin wasn't surprised. She'd seen what Mickey Connor could do. She remembered him tossing Rolf one-handed as if the ninety-pound dog weighed nothing.

"He struck me," Hassan went on, gesturing to the side of his head. "The next thing I remember, I was here and my brother's taxi was gone. He will be very angry with me."

"What's the license plate?" Erin asked.

"Four-B-Nine-Two-B," Hassan said.

"Yellow taxi?"

He nodded.

Erin turned to one of the uniforms. "Call it in. BOLO."

"Copy that," the cop said, keying his radio. He stepped away to give the information to Dispatch.

"Does the cab have GPS?" Erin asked Hassan.

He shook his head. "I do not think so."

"How badly hurt was the big guy?"

"He moved fast, but he was bleeding very much," Hassan said. "I do not think he would die from this wound, but I do not know about such things."

Erin realized she was still holding her Glock at her side. She holstered it and stood up, trying to think what to do next. Maybe they'd get lucky and pick up Hassan's taxi, but she was uncomfortably aware just how many yellow taxis were on the New York streets. Mickey was no idiot. He'd ditch the car or switch its plates at the first opportunity.

Her phone buzzed. It was Webb.

"Are you here?" she asked.

"We just arrived," he said. "But where the hell are you?"

"Around the corner. Mickey beat up a cabbie and stole his car. We just called in the plates, for all the good it'll do."

"You sure it was Connor?"

"Yeah. I'm coming back to the main scene. Be there in a minute." She hung up and pointed to Hassan. "You two take his statement and check him out, see if he needs a doc."

Erin found Vic and Webb examining the two dead guys in the SUV. Vic was looking closely at the shot groupings, lips pursed in a silent whistle of admiration.

"Whoever punched these guys' tickets has one hell of a steady hand," was his opinion.

"It was Ian Thompson," she said.

Vic threw his hands in the air. "Oh, that's just goddamn great. That happy asshole's running around shooting people again? What's that make, four guys he's killed in Manhattan? That we know about? When are we gonna lock this jerkoff up?"

Erin grabbed him by the shoulder and spun him around. Vic was a lot bigger than she was, but she caught him by surprise and off-balance. She pushed him against the side of the SUV.

"That happy asshole, as you call him, took five bullets protecting my family," she snarled. "Five! He's on his way to the hospital right now, if he's even still alive, so shut the hell up!"

"Knock it off, both of you!" Webb snapped.

"What'd I do?" Vic protested.

"Nothing," Erin said. "You haven't done a damn thing except trash-talk the one man who tried to stop my sister getting snatched by a murderous psycho!"

"That's not fair," Vic said. "I got here as fast as I could!"

Erin wanted to hit him. That wasn't quite true. She wanted to hit somebody. Anybody. *Everybody*. She forced herself to take a breath. This wasn't helping Michelle.

"Here's what I know," Webb said, taking advantage of the pause. "We've got one officer dead, another circling the drain, two more bodies right here in front of me, and another guy who's apparently full of holes. Somebody put out a BOLO for a

Michelle O'Reilly, and that doesn't sound like coincidence to me. O'Reilly, start talking. What's going on?"

"We don't have time to screw around," Erin said. "Mickey Connor tried to take out Evan O'Malley at our meeting."

"Why am I just now hearing about this?" Webb demanded.

"There wasn't time. It happened minutes ago, sir. I came straight here from there. He planted a bomb. Rolf found it, Carlyle disarmed it. Nobody got hurt." She was talking very fast. "Mickey figured Carlyle was trying to take him out, but Evan wouldn't okay him hitting Carlyle. Maybe he was already planning to take Evan down and this just sped up his timetable, I don't know. But he knew he had to deal with Evan and Carlyle, and me, too, if he could. So he agreed to this meeting and planted a bomb in the meeting room. And he moved on Shelley at the same time."

"Why her?" Vic asked. "What's she got to do with anything?"

"She's my brother's wife," she said. "I hope she's an insurance policy for Mickey, so he could use her as a hostage if the hit went sideways. Because that means he'll keep her alive. But she got a little tangled up with the O'Malleys."

"How?" Webb asked. "She's a civilian, isn't she?"

"She got involved with James Corcoran," Erin sighed. She didn't want to air her family's dirty laundry, but modesty couldn't take priority over survival.

"So that's the family shit you were talking about?" Vic said. "Damn."

"Connor saw her with him?" Webb asked.

"I think so. Shelley was being followed when she called me up."

"What's Thompson's place in this?"

"Carlyle had him following Mickey. Mickey beat up one of Carlyle's guys last night. We... he thought Mickey might make a move on someone else."

"So Connor came to snatch your sister-in-law and Thompson decided to play white knight?" Vic asked.

"If he intervened to try to prevent a kidnapping, he didn't commit a crime," Erin said. "His gun's legally licensed."

"What about the cops who got shot?" Vic asked.

"Ian wouldn't shoot a cop," she said. "Mickey and his guys must have done that."

"So where do we stand as of this moment?" Webb asked.

"Mickey's got Shelley," Erin said. "Alive, the last anyone knew. He's wounded in the arm but not incapacitated. He's got one accomplice with him and he's in a stolen taxi."

"If he's wounded, he'll need to get treatment," Webb said.

"He won't go to a hospital," Vic said. "He's got to know we'll have his face all over the news. Do you know if the O'Malleys have a doc on retainer?"

"I'll check," she said. "If we move fast enough, maybe—"

"O'Reilly," Webb said softly.

Something in his tone made Erin stop talking and look him in the eye. "What?"

"You can't be on this case," he said. "It's just like me with Catherine Simmons. Remember that? This is your family."

"Damn right it's my family! They're in danger! And I'm going to help them!"

"There's a reason surgeons don't operate on their family," Webb said patiently. "You're compromised."

"There's no compromise here," she said through clenched teeth.

"Let's suppose you find Mickey Connor," he said. "What are you planning to do to him?"

"If he puts his hands in the air and gives up, I'll take him in."

"But you're hoping he doesn't," Webb said.

"What are you talking about, sir?" Vic asked. "Of course Erin needs to be on this case."

Webb turned on him. "Explain," he said coldly.

"She's the one cop in the department with good contacts in the O'Malleys," Vic said. "I don't like it, but the fact is, her being chummy with these guys has an upside right now."

"Evan's people are going to be looking for him, too," Erin said. "And they've got the best idea where he's likely to be. Sir, Ian might have bought us a little time by wounding Mickey, but not much. As soon as he gets treated, he's going to be running, and the second Shelley's no more use to him, he'll... he'll probably kill her."

"Your involvement can poison the case," Webb said.

"I don't give a shit!" Erin snapped. "You think I give a damn about throwing Mickey in jail right now? The important thing is to get Michelle back safe, and to do that, you need me."

"She's right, boss," Vic said.

"I thought you were mad at her," Webb said.

Vic shrugged. "I am. That don't make her wrong, though."

Erin shot him a grateful look. He ignored it.

"Okay," Webb said. "Let's figure out what we're doing. Neshenko, you're sticking with O'Reilly. O'Reilly, find out what you can from your contacts. And I'm afraid you'll need to notify your brother of the situation, if you haven't already. It's just possible Connor may make a ransom demand, or otherwise contact him, and he needs to be prepared. I'll work this scene with CSU and see if we can come up with any useful evidence. I'll notify the FBI and get pictures to the media. Maybe we'll get lucky and somebody will spot them. O'Reilly, do you have a photo of our victim?"

"I'll send you one," she said, taking out her phone again.

"I'll also get in touch with ESU and HRT," Webb said. "If you get a good lead, don't be stupid. Don't be a hero. Make the call and wait for the cavalry. Any questions?"

Erin and Vic shook their heads.

Webb put a hand on Erin's shoulder. "I know this is hard. We'll do everything we can."

"Copy that," she said.

Chapter 11

"Where to first?" Vic asked, sliding into the passenger seat of Erin's Charger.

"The Barley Corner," she said, starting the engine. "Carlyle will be there and so will a lot of his people. They've been bracing for a fight with Mickey's guys, so assume everyone will be packing."

"I always wanted to walk into a Mob bar full of armed thugs," he said. "I just imagined I'd be arresting them, not asking them for help."

"Thanks."

"For what?"

"For having my back with the Lieutenant."

He was surprised. "Of course I've got your back. This is family."

She managed a slight smile. "Vic, you do such a good job acting like an asshole, it's easy to forget what a good guy you can be."

"Don't tell anyone," he said. "I got a rep to protect."

"Sorry I yelled at you. I'm worried about Ian. And he was trying to help."

"Yeah, I get that." Vic shook his head. "And I understand in a comic book, he'd be a hero. But here, in New York, we throw vigilantes in jail."

"He *is* a hero," she insisted. "And if he dies because of this..."

"You really like the guy, don't you."

"Yeah. He's screwed up, but a lot of that is because of the war."

"Like that veteran we busted a while back."

"Yeah."

"That guy tried to kill us," Vic reminded her.

"I know."

"He burned down a movie theater."

"I know."

"And set your dog on fire."

"I know! Give it a rest!"

"Okay, tell you what. For the duration of this case, until your sister-in-law is safe, I promise not to talk any shit about this Thompson punk."

"See, Vic? I said you were a good guy."

He scowled. "Stop rubbing it in. So what do you want to do with Connor once we get him?"

"I told Webb the truth. If he gives up, I'll take him in."

"But what do you *want* to do?" he pressed.

"What do you think? He broke into my family's home, Vic. He grabbed my brother's wife. For all I know, he was after the kids, too. If Ian hadn't been there, he might have all three of them now. I want to gut-shoot him and watch him bleed out screaming. I want him to die slow."

He nodded, satisfied. "That's about what I figured."

"But you still trust me to do this?" she asked.

"Yeah," he said. "Because I know you. You're a bitch, but you're a bitch who tries to do the right thing. You're gonna do this right, 'cause otherwise you wouldn't be able to live with yourself. You want to kill him, but you'll try real hard not to. Besides, I'll be right there with you, watching your six. And if this scumbag tries anything, you better hope you're quicker than me, otherwise I'll be the one putting holes in his guts."

"You know Webb sent you along to keep an eye on me, right?"

He grinned. "I'm not an idiot. I got a brain and it works just fine."

"Isn't this the part where you tell me everything's going to be okay?"

"I'm not gonna bullshit you, Erin. Would you believe me if I said that?"

"No."

"Didn't think so. The only promise I'm making is that I'm with you, all the way."

She blinked her eyes rapidly, trying to clear the tears she felt forming. "Thanks, Vic."

"Forget about it."

"Just let me do the talking with these guys, okay?" she said. "They know me."

"Sure, whatever. Hell, I don't even *want* to talk to them. I'll try to be quiet. Last time I was there, I got in a fistfight. With another cop!"

*   *   *

The Barley Corner was deceptively quiet. A few knots of men were scattered around the main room, talking in low voices. Erin recognized several of Carlyle's guys. She also saw at least three men reach into pockets and under tables when the door opened, then relax when they saw her.

"Hey, Erin," the bartender said.

"Hey, Danny," she replied. "I thought you didn't clock in until evening."

"Mr. Carlyle asked if I wanted to pick up some overtime. Get you anything?"

"I'm working. Where is he?"

"Upstairs. He came in with a couple of kids just a little bit ago. Like, little kids." He held a hand a few feet off the floor to indicate their size.

"Anybody been up to see him?"

"Just Corky."

"That figures. Is he still with him?"

"No, you just missed him."

Erin leaned across the bar and spoke in a lower tone. "How'd Corky look?"

Danny licked his lips. "I don't want to get him in trouble," he said, glancing back and forth between her and Vic.

"We've got bigger fish than Corky to fry," she said.

"You know how he's always smiling?" Danny asked.

She nodded.

"He wasn't."

"Gotcha," she said. "C'mon, Vic. Let's go upstairs. These meatheads down here won't know anything."

"Who you callin' a meathead?" demanded a very large Irishman.

"You resemble that remark?" Vic shot back.

"Take a look in the mirror, buddy," the guy said.

"Lloyd, everybody knows you're a meathead," Erin said to him "Don't take it personally."

Lloyd grinned and rapped his knuckles against his own forehead. "Hey, I knocked a guy out with this head once. I got more than meat in it."

"Don't worry," Erin said in a low voice as she unlocked the door to the upstairs apartment. "If they're insulting you, it means they like you."

"Oh, good. I was gonna lose sleep tonight worrying about whether they liked me," Vic said.

As the door opened, a faint tune wafted down the stairs. It was an Irish tenor singing acapella, an old folk song. It sounded like Carlyle, but Erin realized she hadn't heard him sing before, and now she wondered why not. He had a lovely voice. The tune was one Erin knew as the Scottish song "Loch Lomond," but the words were different.

> *"Red is the rose that in yonder garden grows,*
> *Fair is the lily of the valley,*
> *And clear is the water that flows from the Boyne,*
> *But my love is fairer than any."*

She found Carlyle on the living room couch. Anna was leaning against his left side. Patrick, on his right, lay curled with his head resting on Carlyle's leg, cuddling his sheep. When Carlyle saw the new arrivals, he raised a hand and put a finger to his lips. The children were fast asleep.

Carlyle started another verse as Erin, Vic, and Rolf stood in the doorway.

> *"It's not for the parting that my sister pains,*
> *It's not for the grief of my mother.*
> *It's all for the loss of my bonny Irish lass*
> *That my heart is breaking forever."*

He gently worked himself free from the O'Reilly children, laying them carefully down on the sofa. Then he motioned to the detectives to follow him into his study. He closed the door behind them once they were all inside.

"The poor wee ones had a bit of a shock," he said. "Children often need a nap after something of the sort and I think it's the best thing for them. Any word on their mum?"

"We think Mickey took a bullet," Erin said. "We need to know who the O'Malleys use when they've got a gunshot victim."

Carlyle glanced doubtfully at Vic.

"Vic's okay," she said. "He knows. Everything."

"Was it wise to tell him?" Carlyle asked.

"Nobody told me jack," Vic growled. "I'm a detective, remember? Ever consider I might just be good at my job and figure this shit out?"

"Grand," Carlyle said. "Then we're all on the same side. If Mickey's hurt, he'd likely go to Colin Shaughnessy."

"Who's he?" Erin asked.

"He's a doctor of sports medicine," Carlyle said. "Mickey knows him from his boxing days. But his main income these days comes from trafficking in prescription pills."

"Opioids," Vic said. "Sounds like a real class act."

"He's also known to patch up some of the lads when they get themselves injured," Carlyle said.

"Where does he set up shop?" Erin asked.

"A clinic on West 30th, near the corner of Eighth Avenue, near Madison Square Garden. It's called Joint Adventures."

"Okay," Erin said. "We can be there in twenty minutes."

"He wouldn't have taken your girl to a medical clinic," Vic objected. "If he had another guy with him, he would've had his guy drop him off to get patched up and take her somewhere else."

"But where?" Erin asked. "We have to track Mickey. We find him, we find Shelley."

"Do we want ESU for this?" Vic asked.

"No," she said. "We don't know Mickey's there, and if we have ESU kick down the door, then Evan will know he's got a leak with the NYPD."

"You're still worried about that?" Vic asked.

"She's thinking clearly," Carlyle said. "And we've no need of your Stormtroopers. I can lend you a few lads if you need them."

"What we don't need is a bunch of half-trained gunmen shooting each other in the ass," Vic said.

"They're combat veterans, mates of Ian's," Carlyle said. "As solid as they come."

"We can get Patrol officers if we need more bodies," Erin said.

"Any word on Ian?" Carlyle asked in a softer tone.

She shook her head. "I'll call my brother in a couple minutes. If anyone can tell us, he can. What was Corky doing here?"

"He wanted to help. I think he's gone looking for Mickey."

"Great," Erin muttered. "Just great. So that loose cannon's going to be running around sticking knives in people." "I know how he feels," Carlyle said. "I'd like to be in on this myself."

"You can't," she said. "I know how you feel about Ian and I know what you want to do."

"If you'd let me take care of Mickey earlier, we'd not be in this situation," Carlyle said.

Erin flinched as if he'd slapped her. "Don't," she said, and her voice trembled for the first time in the conversation. "Don't put this on me, just because I stopped you committing *murder*. It's not my fault. It's not your fault. And it sure as shit isn't Shelley's fault."

"Damn right," Vic added. "It's Connor's fault. So, we gonna get this asshole or what?"

Carlyle lowered his eyes. "You're right, darling. I'm sorry. I'm not at my best just now."

She put a hand on his arm. "You're doing great," she said. "And you're helping right here. The kids need you. Let me do what I do."

"As you wish, darling. I'll keep my ear to the street. Shall I call you with any news?"

"Yeah," she said. "I'll have my phone on me. And I'll call you about Ian. You're right, too, Vic. We'd better move, and move fast."

"How about calling ahead?" Vic suggested. "We can have a couple Patrol units down the street. That way we'll know if he comes or goes."

"Good idea," she said. "But they have to keep their distance. If Mickey gets spooked, it'll put Shelley in more danger."

Carlyle offered Vic his hand. "Look after her, lad," he said.

Vic stared at the hand. "I'm not shaking your hand," he said. "And I'm not doing any of this for you. But don't worry. I got this."

Chapter 12

Erin didn't want to have the upcoming conversation in front of Vic. In fact, she didn't want to have it at all. But she had very little choice. They were on a clock and it was something that needed to be done. She tried to get comfortable behind the wheel of her Charger, buckled her seatbelt, and called the hospital. She got through the usual automated menu instructing her to call 911 for an emergency, to push various buttons to make appointments or talk to different departments. She'd done this dance before. She finally got through to the phone in the emergency room.

"Bellevue Hospital emergency room," a nurse said. No pleasant receptionist here, just a tough-sounding woman taking care of business.

"Can you page Dr. O'Reilly, please?" Erin said, putting the car in gear.

"Dr. O'Reilly is in surgery," the nurse said. "Would you like to leave a callback number?"

"This is his sister," she said. "It's a family emergency. Do you know if he's actually in the OR right now?"

"I'll check. One moment."

Erin drove north, listening to hold music and trying to think what she could possibly tell her brother. Vic was trying to be polite, looking out the window and acting like he couldn't hear her. Rolf circled in his compartment, panting. He could feel her nerves and it was making him tense.

The music cut off and the nurse was back. "I'll connect you," she said. There was a click of a transfer, then another ring.

"Erin?" her brother said. "Make this quick. I'm just scrubbing in. I'm really busy, we've got multiple GSW cases here. They said you've got an emergency."

"Sean..." she began. She swallowed the lump in her throat. This was one of the hardest things she'd ever had to say.

"Erin? What is it?" His voice lost its briskness and took on a note of concern. "Oh God, is it Dad? Mom?"

"It's... it's Shelley, Sean. She's been taken."

"What? What do you mean, taken? What's wrong with Shelley?"

"We think she's all right, for now. But some men attacked your house. We think she's been kidnapped." Erin realized, belatedly, what a bad idea it had been to have this talk while trying to drive. She blinked rapidly to clear her vision and tried to pay enough attention to the road so she didn't run into anybody.

"Kidnapped?" he repeated blankly.

"Sean, I'm so sorry," she said. "And I promise, I will do absolutely everything I can to get her back. The kids are fine, Sean. Anna and Patrick are just fine. They're back at my place. I called Dad and he and Mom are on their way. But the guys who took her might try to contact you. We'll have a negotiator get in touch with you, so you know what to do. You've got my commander's number, right? Harry Webb?"

"Yeah, I think so." Sean sounded dazed, like he'd been hit over the head.

"He's at my station. He can help with any questions you've got, so call him if you need someone in the Department. We don't know a lot yet."

"Do they want money? Shelley's got... we've got money. Whatever it takes, we'll pay it. I just... I need her back safe. Who did this? Who the hell did this?"

"I know who's responsible and I'm going to find him." Heartbreak was fighting it out with anger in Erin. The anger was winning.

"You're sure the kids are okay?" Sean asked. "You've seen them?"

"Yeah, they're fine. Like I said, they're at my place. My boyfriend's watching them until our folks get there."

"Oh, God," he said. "What am I going to tell them? I should've been there. I could've done something."

"Sean, this isn't your fault. You wouldn't have been able to stop this guy. Two cops and one of... one of my friends tried. They all got shot. If you'd been there, you would've been shot, too."

"This friend of yours," Sean said, pulling himself a little together. "Super fit, short haircut, tattoos on his arm?"

"Yeah, that's him," she said. "How do you—?"

"He's waiting in my OR right now," he said. "Jesus Christ."

"How is he?" Erin asked, knowing Sean had too many other things to worry about, but unable to stop herself.

"The EMTs got him stabilized in the ambulance," he said. As he fell back into his medical training, his voice steadied a little. "And we've been working on him, getting the bleeding stopped. He's had four units of blood pumped into him. We just prepped him for surgery. He's been shot five times, and that's never good, but only two of them are really serious. I won't know about internal damage until I go in. I'd better... God, I'd better get in there. I don't know if I can do this."

"Just do your job," she said. "You can't help Shelley right now, but you can help Ian. Save lives, big brother. That's what you do."

"Oh, God," Sean said again.

"Keep it together," she said. "You've got this."

"You'll let me know if... if you... if anything..."

"I'll call you," she promised. "I love you, Junior."

"I love you, kiddo," he said in a dull, broken voice. Then he hung up.

Erin drove in silence for about thirty seconds. Then, quietly, she said what she was thinking.

"I'm going to kill that son of a bitch."

She thought Vic might protest or disagree, but he didn't say anything. They went the rest of the way without another word.

*   *   *

"This isn't a drug den," Vic said when they got there.

"I know that," Erin said.

"It's not a meth lab. Or a gang headquarters."

Erin swung the Charger into a police space a few yards down the street from Joint Adventures and turned to face him. "What's your point, Vic?"

"My point is, we can't just kick down the door and arrest everybody, and you sure as hell can't shoot up the Downtown."

"Never thought I'd hear you say that."

"I know you're upset, Erin."

"I'm upset."

"Yeah."

"You could say that."

"So I want to make sure you don't go flying off the handle. You don't want to do something you'll regret."

"I'm totally calm."

He didn't believe her. She didn't care.

Erin took Rolf into the waiting room, Vic on her heels. The room was clean and well-lit, the walls painted a white so bright it almost sparkled. Aside from a security camera in the corner, it was a cheerful, welcoming place. As drug-dealing fronts went, it was pretty upscale. The receptionist was attractively but conservatively dressed, a thirtysomething woman with a friendly smile.

"Good afternoon, ma'am," she said. "Sir. What can I help you with today?"

"I'm here to see Dr. Shaughnessy," Erin said. "I don't have an appointment."

"I'm sorry, Dr. Shaughnessy is seeing another patient right now. We aren't usually able to accommodate walk-ins. But if you'd like to make an appointment, I can give you some forms to fill out now. We have some openings early next week."

Erin laid her shield on the counter. "Detective O'Reilly, Major Crimes," she said. "This can't wait."

The receptionist's smile faltered. "I see," she said. "I'm terribly sorry, but the doctor really is unavailable at the moment. This appointment should wrap up sometime in the next twenty to thirty minutes."

"Now," Erin said. She started for the door that led into the facility.

"Ma'am, there's no need to be rude," the woman said. "You can't just barge in here without a warrant."

Erin ignored her and kept walking.

"I'll make one phone call," the receptionist said. Her smile was only a memory now. "And you'll be in so much trouble, you won't know what hit you."

Erin paused. "Make that call," she said. "I can even tell you who to call. Call Evan O'Malley and tell him Erin O'Reilly's here about Mickey. See what he says."

The receptionist's mouth dropped open. Before she could think of a reply, Erin pushed through the door.

"This is you being totally calm?" Vic said conversationally. "I kinda like it. It's hot. Reminds me of Zofia."

"We don't have time to screw around," she said.

"That lady's right," Vic added. "We haven't got a warrant. Anything we find here is an illegal search. Inadmissible."

"You think I care about that? You heard Carlyle. Mickey's safer in jail than on the outside. I don't give a damn if he gets locked up or not. As long as we get Shelley back, he can go wherever he wants. Preferably straight to hell."

She saw a door labeled EXAMINATION. A faint voice was audible on the other side. She looped Rolf's leash around her left wrist, took hold of the doorknob with that hand, and wrapped the other around the grip of her Glock. Vic had hold of his own sidearm. He nodded to her.

She twisted the knob and pushed the door open, stepping quickly in and to the side, clearing Vic's field of fire. Two men were in the room, one sitting, the other standing. The standing one was medium height, overweight, clad in a white lab coat. The seated guy was enormous, tremendous shoulders straining against a tight T-shirt, a bullet-shaped head anchored to his shoulders by a neck so thick it didn't taper at all. But it wasn't Mickey Connor. The big guy looked vaguely familiar. Erin thought she might have seen him on TV. He was some sort of professional athlete.

The man in the coat spun around. His face went from surprise to annoyance. "How did you get in here?" he snapped in a reedy, petulant voice. "This is a private consultation!"

"NYPD Major Crimes," Erin shot back, holding up her shield in her left hand. She kept her right ready to reach for her gun, just in case. There were no hiding places big enough for Mickey in the room, but she was taking no chances.

"What's the problem, doc?" the big guy asked. His voice was deep, low, and deceptively soft, but he stood up as he spoke.

"Back off, pal," Vic advised. "You don't want any part of this."

The two men considered one another. The big guy—Erin was sure now he was a football player, but couldn't place his name—had two inches on Vic and looked like he knew how to handle himself. But something in Vic's eye and posture warned the man that this was no time for macho bullshit. The guy backed down.

"I don't know what you think you're doing here," the doctor said, "but you're going to have to leave. You can't harass me in front of my patients."

"Where's Mickey Connor?" Erin demanded.

"I don't know what you're talking about," Shaughnessy said.

"So if I check the feed from your security cameras for the last couple hours, I won't see him on the tapes?"

"You need a court order for those," Shaughnessy protested.

"He's right, Vic," Erin said. "I do need a court order for those, unless he voluntarily provides the footage."

"Showing you that footage would be a HIPAA violation," Shaughnessy said. "It would illegally invade my patients' privacy."

"Right again," Erin said. "But I don't need to see the footage if you answer my damn question. Where's Mickey Connor? I know he was here. Is he still here?"

She was advancing on him as she spoke. Rolf, at her hip, stared at the doctor intently, watching and waiting for instructions. Shaughnessy backed away.

"This is outrageous!" he said. "I don't have to tell you anything!"

Erin got right in his face. She took hold of his lapels and pulled herself in close. They were eyeball to eyeball. She let him see just how angry she was, gave him a second to understand.

"Doc—" the football player started to say.

"Why don't you wait in the lobby?" Vic suggested. The other man thought about it and decided this was a good time to be somewhere else. He left.

"He came in with a bullet wound," Erin said, speaking quietly but with no hint of softness. "You didn't report it to the police, as you're required by law to do. You took care of him, no questions asked. He paid you in cash. I don't give a damn about any of that, just like I don't give a damn about the narcotics you peddle under the table. Here's what I do care about: Mickey tried to blow up Evan O'Malley at noon today. I know, because I was there. My name's Erin O'Reilly, I'm Cars Carlyle's personal attack dog, and if I don't find Mickey, I'm going to drop so much shit on your head, you'll drown in it. Mickey's going down. You can go down with him, or you can give me what I want, and we both walk away winners."

Shaughnessy's eyes were very wide. He stared at her, his mouth working. In his eyes was recognition of who she was and what she represented. He wasn't scared that she was a cop; he was scared of Evan and Carlyle.

"What's it going to be?" Erin asked. "This offer is good for a limited time only."

Shaughnessy tried to say something. He managed only a dry rasp. He cleared his throat, licked his lips, and tried again.

"Please," he whispered. "I can't squeal on Mickey. I got a wife and kid."

"Mickey's got my brother's wife," she snapped. "And they've got two kids wondering whether their mommy's going to come home. Mickey's not your problem. I am."

"He's not here."

"I know that. But he was."

Shaughnessy nodded.

"When?" Erin demanded.

"He left about an hour ago," Shaughnessy said. "I told him I needed more time, but he was in a hurry, so I just did a quick patch-up job."

"How bad was he hit?" she asked.

"He'd been shot once, in the left forearm. He'd lost some blood, but it was just muscle damage. The bullet missed the bone. I gave him some painkillers and stitched up the hole."

"Anything else?"

"A couple grams of coke. He said he needed something to keep him going, pick him up from the narcotics."

"Can he use the arm?" she asked.

"If he has to. It'll hurt, but he's not disabled."

"Where did he go?"

"How the hell am I supposed to know that?" Shaughnessy asked, summoning up a little backbone. "He didn't tell me!"

"How did he leave?"

"He went out the back. He had a car in the alley."

"What kind of car?"

"Taxi, I think. Yellow."

"Did you get a look at the license plate?"

He shook his head. Erin wasn't surprised. In the Life, it was better not to notice things like that.

"Was anybody else in the car?" she asked.

Shaughnessy thought about it. Then he nodded. "Yes, I saw a man and a woman in the back seat."

Erin let out her breath. Michelle had been there, only a little while ago. But they'd missed her again.

"That's all I know," Shaughnessy said.

"Did you notice anything about him?" Erin asked. "Stains on his clothes? Powder? Dust?"

"Bloodstains," the doctor said. "But nothing else you could see... oh. There was a smell."

"What smell?"

"Mickey had kind of a rusty smell, like old metal, with a little bit of something else. Burnt sugar, maybe? I wasn't sure of it, on account of the fresh blood. But that's all. I swear."

"One other thing," she said. "When you patched him up, you must have used surgical pads to mop up the blood."

"Of course." Shaughnessy gave her a very strange look. "What does that have to do with anything?"

"I need one of them."

"What for?"

"What do you care?"

Shaughnessy pointed to a covered bin with a biohazard warning on it. Vic put on a pair of disposable gloves, opened the lid, and gingerly took out a blood-soaked gauze pad. He produced an evidence bag from a pocket and slipped it in.

"I did what you wanted!" Shaughnessy protested. "You don't have a warrant. This is an illegal search. You can't use that in court!"

"I don't plan to," she said. Then she led Rolf out of the room. Vic followed.

Chapter 13

"Now what?" Vic asked.

Erin gripped the steering wheel and scowled at the dashboard. She didn't know.

"He's got his first aid," Vic went on. "So he's not going to a hospital. But that's gotta slow him down a little. He knows Old Man O'Malley's looking for him, so he won't be at any of his usual spots."

"I know that!" Erin snapped. "Shut up for a second and let me think!"

Vic shot her a look, but he closed his mouth.

Erin knew he was right. Mickey was in a tight spot. He was injured and he'd tried to kill his boss. A cornered man was a dangerous man. But a cornered man was also predictable.

"He's only got three choices," she said slowly. "Run, fight, or hide."

"Yeah," Vic said. "The smart play is to get as far from New York as he can. How much reach does O'Malley have?"

"Evan's a New York gangster," she said. "If Mickey puts a couple of state lines between him and Evan, he might get away, assuming he keeps his head down. But if he turns up in, say,

Chicago six months from now, Evan will send guys after him. O'Malley can't afford to let this slide."

Vic nodded. "Is this Connor punk the type to lie low and keep out of the spotlight?"

"No," she said. "And he's not the running type, either."

"You don't think he'll beat feet out of Manhattan?"

"He might go as far as Long Island, or maybe Jersey, but no farther. He knows this town and I don't think he plans on leaving."

"Then he'll hide or he'll fight," Vic said. "And you just said he's not the sort of guy who's content to duck and cover."

"If he drops out of sight, it's a temporary tactical move," she said. "He won't stay down forever. No, Mickey's got to take Evan out as soon as possible. That's his only move."

"So why's he still holding your sister-in-law? O'Malley doesn't give a shit about her."

"But I do, and that means Carlyle does. Maybe he's planning on using her as a bargaining chip to make Carlyle set up Evan."

"Carlyle's smarter than that," Vic objected. "He's got to know if Connor takes over, he's next on that asshole's list."

"That's the first time I've heard you pay Carlyle a compliment."

"I never said he wasn't smart. Plenty of jerks are smart."

"Mickey's whole endgame is to wipe out his opponents in the O'Malleys," she said. "He knows Evan won't ever forgive him, just like he knows I won't ever stop coming after him for grabbing Shelley."

Vic nodded. "He's going to be coming after you," he said. "That's why he's holding her. She's bait."

"That and he's a sadistic bastard," she said bitterly. "He likes hurting women. We've got to get her back, or she's dead."

"If he knows you know that, he can set you up, draw you in," Vic said. "But he's got to know you won't be alone. And we'll come heavy. If he thinks he can win a gunfight with ESU, he's out of his damn mind."

"Mickey's no gunfighter. He's a boxer. He works up close and personal, one on one. He'll try to maneuver me into doing something stupid, making myself vulnerable. Then he'll hit me."

"That's why I'm here," Vic said. "To make sure you don't do anything stupid. But where is he?"

"Rust and burnt sugar," Erin mused.

"Come again?"

"The doctor said Mickey smelled like rust and burnt sugar."

"That's no surprise," Vic said. "The guy was shot. He had blood leaking out of him. Blood smells like metal."

"What about the sugar?" she replied. "I think he's hiding out somewhere that smells like that."

"So now we're canvassing neighborhoods based on scratch and sniff?" Vic said dubiously. "I swear, you get more like your K-9 every day. I dunno, Erin. There's one hell of a lot of Manhattan out there, and a lot of it's covered with rust."

"Not much smells like burnt sugar, though," she said. "I think we're looking for a sugar plant or a candy factory. Not a new one. A derelict."

"But he smelled like where he'd been, not where he was going."

"I think he was setting up a hideout ahead of time. If I had to guess, he came from there straight to Junior's house and he's going right back."

"That's one hell of a logical jump," he said. "You know what Webb would say."

"Thin, I know," she said. "But it's all we've got."

"You're going on a smell you didn't even smell yourself!"

"Do you have a better idea?"

"I wish I did, because this idea is crap. So what do you want to do? Look up all the shuttered sugar shops in town? I don't think the NYPD has a database for that."

Erin took out her phone. "I think we can narrow it down a little," she said, calling Carlyle's number.

"What news, darling?" he asked, almost before the first ring had ended.

"Do you know any old factories in O'Malley territory?" she asked. "Ones that used to manufacture candy?"

"Perhaps," he said. "Corky's better on that sort of thing. I'll give him a call and see what he knows. Anything else you can tell me?"

"It's a place that would make a guy smell like burnt sugar and rust," she said. "That's all I could think of."

"I'll ring you back. I'm guessing any such place would be in Brooklyn or Queens, rather than Manhattan."

"Okay, thanks. Ian made it to the hospital. My brother's working on him right now."

"Will he pull through?"

"Too early to tell," she said. "But Junior's the best they've got."

"I know, darling," he said. "I'm carrying the marks of his handiwork, in case you've forgotten. I'll ring you back in a few minutes."

She hung up and started the car. "We're heading south," she announced.

"You don't even know where you're going yet," Vic said.

"Mickey's on Long Island," she said with more certainty than she felt. It was more gut feeling than anything, but when all you had to go on was your gut, it was a hell of a lot better than nothing.

"So you want to get close," he said. "Fine by me. We alerting HRT?"

"And tell them what?" she replied. "That I'm playing a hunch based on smell? Didn't you just laugh that off?"

"Nobody's laughing, Erin. But you're right. We need more. Hell, we won't even have a warrant. We've got no PC. What are you planning on doing, assuming we even find the right place?"

"I'll figure that out once we get there."

*   *   *

They'd made it to the Lower East Side of Manhattan by the time Erin's phone rang. She glanced down, saw Carlyle's number, and swiped the screen, putting the call on speaker.

"Give me good news," she said.

"Try the Domino Sugar Refinery in Brooklyn," Carlyle said.

"Of course! What did you hear about it?" Erin felt foolish for not tumbling to that possibility herself. She'd seen that building. It was iconic, a massive brick factory that lay just north of the Williamsburg Bridge. She'd passed it on the way into Manhattan more than once.

"It's been closed since aught-four," he said. "Some community organization purchased it, with the intention of gentrifying the area, but that effort's been languishing. In the meantime, according to Corky, it's a handy place to stock certain items for transport across the East River. You'll find a number of stash locations within, if you've some idea where to look. I don't know of any O'Malley lads there at present, but it's definitely part of our territory."

"Sounds perfect," she said.

"It's not one of Mickey's usual haunts," he added.

"Even better. If Evan was gunning for you, would you hang around the Corner?"

"Excellent point, darling."

"Just how big is this place?" Vic asked.

"It's large," Carlyle said. "And it's falling apart. If you go in, you'll want to be cautious and mind your head."

"Has anyone heard anything about Mickey?" Erin asked.

"Only rumors. A few of his lads have gone missing, too."

"How many?"

"Hard to say. We don't take roll call the way your lot do. But I expect he has four or five lads about him. Discounting the two he lost in Midtown, I'd say two or three are likely to be close to hand."

"Okay, thanks. If you think of another place he might be, let me know."

"You'll be the first, darling. And remember, should you encounter him face to face, he's faster than he looks."

"I'm not likely to forget."

*   *   *

They could see the factory from the Williamsburg Bridge, just on the left as they crossed into Brooklyn. A single gigantic smokestack thrust up from a pile of crumbling brick. Scaffolding sheathed the dilapidated walls in an effort to keep the building as upright as possible. Row upon row of windows, most of them intact, a few broken and gaping, stared glassily across the East River.

"Holy shit," Vic said. "That thing's huge."

"I think my dad once told me a thousand guys worked there," Erin said.

"If Kira Jones were here, she'd be able to tell us how many, and for how long," he said.

"We could use her right now," she said.

"Speaking of which," Vic said. "You given any thought to calling in some backup?"

"We'll take a look around," she said. "If we see any sign Mickey's inside, then we'll call the cavalry. But there's no point hauling ESU on a wild goose chase."

Erin headed north on Kent Avenue. The factory was just two blocks ahead. She kept the Charger's speed down and didn't use the lights or siren. The very last thing they wanted to do was tip Mickey off that they were coming. She turned onto a cul-de-sac just short of the factory and stopped the car.

"You got the blood?" she asked.

Vic held up the evidence bag with the bloodstained gauze. "Right here."

"I should've gotten something of Shelley's," she said, mad at herself for forgetting.

"Hey, if we find that asshole, she's sure to be close by," he said. "And if we take him out of circulation, she's got nothing to worry about. Got your vest?" He reached for the rifle rack and pulled out Erin's AR-15. He gave the rifle a quick once-over and pulled the charging lever, chambering a round.

"Yeah." Erin stepped out of the car and opened Rolf's compartment. "*Bleib*," she told the K-9, who held still while she fastened him into his own body armor.

"You gonna be good with just that peashooter?" he asked, pointing to the Glock on her hip.

"I've got my backup piece, too," she said.

"Never understood why you don't like long guns. A rifle's a lot better. More accurate, better stopping power. I'd never go in with just a handgun if I had the choice."

"That's because you don't have to hold a dog. Try shooting a rifle one-handed."

"Good point. You ready for this?"

"Ready when you are."

"You understand we can't legally go in without PC."

"Let's do a quick walk-around and see what's going on," she suggested.

"Keep close to the wall," he advised. "That way if anyone's looking out the windows, he'll have trouble seeing us."

They started in a circuit around the building. On the west side of the factory, between River Street and the East River, was a strip of parkland. A few pedestrians were walking along the riverbank. Some of them noticed the detectives in their POLICE-labeled vests, Vic with rifle in hand, and paused to watch. Erin ignored them, hoping they had the sense to keep clear of the situation if it turned nasty.

The west wall of the building was a row of loading docks with sliding doors. The area was littered with trash, the concrete showing colorful splashes of graffiti. Only one thing was out of place in the landscape of urban decay.

"Oh, shit," she said.

"What?" Vic demanded. "What is it?"

She stared at the bright yellow BMW convertible parked in the shadow of the factory by the loading dock. She knew that car. Not only did she know who owned it, she'd driven it once herself.

"Corky's here," she said, starting around the corner.

"Corcoran? What the hell for?"

"Carlyle got this location from him," she said. "Either he told Corky why he wanted to know, or Corky guessed. Corky's coming after Mickey."

"Why? Does he have a personal beef with Connor? Or is he just eager to get whacked?"

"You're right, he doesn't care about danger," Erin said. "But he's here because of Shelley." She saw another car next to the BMW, but it wasn't a yellow taxi. It was a blue Ford Escort. Maybe Mickey had changed vehicles. Maybe it had nothing to do with them at all.

"Just great," Vic said. "Another goddamn white knight. These idiots are all gonna get themselves killed."

Erin put out a hand and levered herself onto the concrete loading dock. "*Hupf!*" she said in a low voice. Rolf scrambled up beside her. The corrugated sliding door was raised a couple of feet, leaving an opening.

Vic clambered up to join them. "What's Corcoran gonna do?" he asked.

"I don't know," she said. "But knowing him, something crazy."

"Is this our problem?"

"It is if it puts Mickey on guard," she said. "If he knows he's been found, he might just kill Shelley and make a run for it."

"Damn," Vic said. "I knew I should've stayed in bed this morning. We going in without a warrant?"

"I'll take the responsibility," she said.

"I'm a big boy. You don't have to protect me."

"I'm not asking you to go in with me."

"I'm not asking your permission."

Erin drew her Glock and checked the chamber, making sure it was loaded. Then she ducked under the door into the factory.

The loading bay was filthy, the floor covered with debris. The ceiling was a patchy mess of falling plaster, rusting pipes, and exposed wiring. Big support columns marched in rows across the space. The lighting was dim, but enough sunlight filtered through the windows that she didn't need her flashlight.

"What a shit-heap," Vic said.

"Give me the blood," she said, holding out her hand.

He passed over the evidence bag. She opened it and held it in front of Rolf's snout.

"Rolf. *Such!*" she ordered.

The Shepherd's nostrils twitched, taking in the scent of Mickey's fresh blood. He raised his nose and sniffed the air, tail waving. Then, as if an electric shock had run down his spine, he stiffened and started moving deeper into the building.

"Screw this," Vic said. "His snout's enough proof for me. I'm calling backup."

"Tell them to come quiet," Erin said as she set off after her dog. "No sirens."

"Dispatch," Vic said into his phone. "Detective Neshenko, shield six-niner-niner-two. Requesting backup at the Domino Sugar Refinery, Brooklyn. Whatever you've got in the area. A couple Patrol units at least. We have two detectives on scene. Possible hostage situation. Be discreet. Tell them to come quietly."

Rolf was on a mission, forging ahead, throwing his shoulders against the tension of his leash. Erin felt a mounting excitement. The K-9 was on a good, fresh trail. Mickey was here, or at least he'd been here not long ago. Maybe there was still time. But what was Corky up to? She'd have to make sure she didn't shoot him by mistake.

Up ahead, somewhere in the shadowy depths of the factory, there was a sudden rattle of noise, a blast of gunfire and the smack of bullets into brick. Somebody cried out in surprise, or maybe pain.

"10-13!" Vic barked into his phone. "Domino Sugar Refinery! Shots fired! Forget being sneaky. Tell them to get their asses over here!"

Erin started running.

"Erin! Wait for the backup!" Vic hissed.

But Erin didn't listen. The backup wouldn't get there in time. She ran toward the sound of the shooting.

Chapter 14

The shots echoed hollowly in the building, making it difficult to tell where they were coming from. The gun had the popping sound of subsonic pistol rounds, rather than the flat crack of rifle cartridges, so Erin guessed it was a submachine-gun. She thought the fire was above her and a little to the north, exactly the way Rolf was headed.

The K-9 led the way to the foot of a rickety metal stairway. He lunged up the steps, still hot on the scent. Erin was right there with him, pistol in hand. She heard the heavy thud of Vic's feet pounding close behind.

Rolf hit a door and scrabbled at it with his claws, whining. Erin looped his leash around her wrist, grabbed the door handle with that hand, and flung it open. The room was the terminus of a conveyor belt that ran through a passage in the north wall, slanting downhill into the main building.

Rolf tugged toward the conveyor belt, which was now just a line of metal rollers, the belt itself having rotted away. A walkway ran alongside it. They raced that direction as another volley of shots echoed in the darkness ahead of them.

Erin reached the bottom of the conveyor belt and burst onto the floor of the old factory. The soles of her shoes made crackling, sticky sounds and clung to the floor. She thought of movie theaters and spilled soda pop. Pools of dark, melted sugar lay across the floor like a weird, industrial swamp. Enormous rusty machines loomed all around. It was very dark, a shadowy maze of metal. Rolf knew where he was going, but she paused a second to get her bearings. As she fumbled for her flashlight, Vic caught up with her.

"No," he said in a low voice. "Don't show a light. They'll see you better than you can see them."

She nodded her understanding. Then, right on the other side of one of the machines, the submachine-gun fired again.

"Missed me that time, scunner," Corky's unmistakable voice sang out tauntingly.

"I'll get you with the next one," an unfamiliar man's voice called back.

"*Fuss*," Erin hissed to Rolf, telling him to heel. He immediately stopped pulling and looked at her for further instructions.

Vic pointed to himself, then the far corner of the machine, indicating he'd go around the back and try to outflank the shooter. Erin nodded and pointed to herself and Rolf. Then she pointed the direction Mickey's trail led. They couldn't afford to get pinned down shooting it out with one of Mickey's goons.

She led Rolf, quickly and quietly, along the side wall. "*Such!*" she whispered to the dog, re-engaging his search protocol.

He nosed forward at once, pulling toward a door in the wall in front of her. She reached for it.

"NYPD, asshole!" Vic snapped behind her. "Drop it!"

His voice was drowned out by gunfire. Vic cursed. Then his rifle cracked three times in rapid succession. The submachine-gun fired again. Corky shouted something.

Erin was momentarily torn. Her training told her to help her fellow detective, but her gut told her Michelle was in danger too. She had to trust Vic and Corky to take care of whatever was at her back. She took a breath and lunged through the door.

She found herself in a locker room. Rows of rusty metal lockers still lined the walls and formed an island in the middle of the room next to a circular wash-basin, just like she remembered from her elementary school days. Old insulation, dust, and cobwebs hung in gray streamers from the ceiling. The basin was dry and coated with a thick layer of dust.

Rolf pulled between two rows of lockers, panting hard. Erin followed. The Shepherd came to the end of the lockers and angled to the right.

He gave a short, sharp bark that turned into a yelp of surprised pain. The dog tumbled backward, skidding on the dusty floor, scrambling to regain his footing.

In that moment, Erin knew what was coming. She'd been expecting it ever since she'd entered the factory. She flicked her wrist, dropping Rolf's leash, and wrapped her left hand around her right, bringing up the Glock in a two-handed Weaver stance. "*Fass!*" she shouted to Rolf.

Mickey Connor came around the corner.

Most big guys were slow on their feet, but Mickey had been a professional boxer, and boxers were *fast*. He'd gained some weight since his prizefighting days, but he was still much quicker than anyone his size had any right to be. He moved like the star athlete he'd been, and he ran straight at her with unbelievable speed.

His hands were curled into fists, no weapon she could see, but he was less than ten feet away and closing. She didn't waste time identifying herself or telling him to stop. He already knew who she was, and she might as well order an onrushing freight train to halt.

Erin fired twice, as fast as she could pull the trigger, aiming straight for his center of mass. The shots punched into Mickey's chest. He didn't slow down, gave no sign he even knew he'd been shot. She shifted aim, going for a head shot.

Mickey's left fist looped in, catching her on the right arm just below the shoulder. It was like being hit with a sledgehammer. The impact was so hard it went beyond pain, overloading her nerves. She felt only a tremendous, jarring shock to the bone and then her whole arm went numb. The pistol spun out of her hand and skittered across the floor.

Erin tried to duck, tried to backpedal away, but Mickey's right hand was already in motion. A short, vicious right hook crashed into the side of her head.

Brilliant starbursts exploded in Erin's eyes. She went momentarily blind and deaf, a curious feeling of weightlessness lifting her clear of the ground. She was floating, not falling, conscious only of a sudden rush of coppery liquid in her mouth.

Too fast, she thought disjointedly. *He's too damn fast.* She blinked, trying to clear her vision, and saw a blurry silhouette in front of her, drawing back an arm that looked like a tree limb. She heard a snarl, a feral, ferocious noise. Maybe it was her own voice, a last defiant growl.

Mickey faltered and stumbled as Rolf leaped back into the fight, the K-9's jaws snapping shut on the man's upraised forearm. Rolf bit down with all his force.

Mickey roared a curse and swung his arm. Rolf weighed every ounce of ninety pounds, but the enormous man tossed the Shepherd around like a rag-doll. Rolf had tangled with Mickey once before and had lost his grip on that occasion. But he was ready now, itching for a rematch. The K-9 wasn't letting go, not this time.

Erin realized she was sitting down, her back against something hard and metallic. How had that happened? She didn't remember sitting or falling. Her thoughts were mushy and muddled. She put down a hand, braced herself on the floor, and tottered up on her knees. Rolf couldn't win this fight on his own. She knew she should remember something, something important, but she just couldn't think clearly.

Mickey slammed Rolf into the lockers with a tremendous, echoing clang. The Shepherd kept growling and hung on like grim death. Mickey pulled back and did it again, then a third time. Rolf's snarl cut off. The dog's jaws suddenly relaxed. He slid off Mickey's arm and fell to the filthy floor in a limp, furry heap.

Erin wanted to scream, but her mouth didn't seem to be working properly. It was full of blood and her tongue felt too big for it. Mickey turned back to her. He was smiling a savage grin that showed his teeth. Blood streamed down his arm in a sheet from Rolf's bite, but he didn't care. That arm was angled funny, probably broken. He had blood all over him. He should be dead but he wasn't. Maybe he wasn't even human.

Her ankle gun. That was what she'd been trying to think of. Erin let her hand fall to the top of her shoe, feeling for the handle of the little snub-nosed revolver.

Mickey opened his left hand. A roll of coins fell from it, splitting and spilling across the floor in a shower of silver. He'd been using it as a fist-load to add extra power to his punches. Now the massive hand fit easily around Erin's neck. He lifted her clear off the floor without apparent effort, bringing their faces close together.

Her vision cleared, just for a moment. She saw pale, empty blue eyes, bloodshot from drugs; a broken nose, dusted with white powder; a mouth, lips drawn tight in a victorious grimace.

Her fingers closed around the pistol. She tugged it out of the holster.

"Try to kill me, bitch?" he growled. "I'm gonna make you scream."

Erin spat a mouthful of blood full in his face. Mickey cursed and flinched. Erin brought up her hand, shoving the muzzle of the .38 under his chin. She pulled the trigger.

There was a tremendous noise, the loudest clap of thunder she'd ever heard. Then, nothing.

* * *

Erin saw bright, featureless white. Was she dead? Maybe this was what heaven looked like. She blinked. Her eyelids went up and down. The world went dark, then bright again. That meant her eyes were working. She became conscious of an intense, pounding headache, like the worst hangover she'd ever felt. There couldn't be hangovers in heaven, could there? Maybe she'd ended up in the other place. Her stomach lurched. She made a semi-coherent noise and reached for something, anything. Somebody put a thing in her hand, some kind of container. She bent her head over it and emptied her stomach, vomiting so hard the pain in her head redoubled.

She wiped at her mouth with a shaking hand. "Where am I?" she asked thickly.

"Bellevue Hospital," a familiar voice at her elbow said. She couldn't place it immediately, so she turned to look and immediately wished she hadn't. Her neck was very stiff and her head felt fragile, like it might shatter.

Vic was sitting next to the bed, trying not to look worried. The expression of half-guarded concern was so out of place on his face that Erin wondered for a second whether she was really awake. Something seemed to have happened to his shirt. The only thing he had on his chest was his undershirt, dirty and sweat-stained.

"What happened?" she asked.

"You don't remember?" he replied. "Yeah, I guess you wouldn't. You got a pretty good knock on the head. But you were awake for some of it at least. Weird. The doc said you might have some trouble putting things together. Jesus, that big bastard really rang your bell."

"Vic?"

"Yeah?" He leaned closer.

She formed the words carefully, enunciating each one. "Tell me what happened. That's an order."

"Oh. Right." He cleared his throat. "After I got done with those other two losers, I heard shooting. And your dog was growling. So I told Corcoran to keep an eye on those sons of bitches and came running. Found you lying under that sorry sack of shit Connor, practically flattened. Your mutt was clamped on his arm, trying to haul him off you, and he just wouldn't let go. So I gave him a hand and hefted the asshole off you. What was left of him, anyway."

"Is Mickey dead?"

"You blew the top of his head clean off. Hell yeah, he's dead. Powder burns under the chin. You must've been contact close."

"Shelley," Erin said, remembering. "Did you find Shelley?"

"She's fine," he said. "It's okay. I got her. She's here, just down the hall."

"Did he... hurt her?"

Vic shook his head. "She's pretty shook up, but nothing serious. They just brought her in as a precaution."

"How'd you find her?"

"I was getting to that. By the time I got that lard-ass's body off you—shit, that guy really weighed a ton—we had a whole bunch of cops showing up, medics right behind them. But your crazy dog wouldn't let any of them near you. I was the only one he'd let touch him, so I had to hold him back while they got you up on a stretcher."

"How is he?"

"Rolf? I dropped him at the vet. They said he had a concussion and maybe some cracked ribs. About like you. I notice you haven't asked how bad you're hurt."

"Oh. How bad am I hurt?"

"How the hell do I know that? Do I look like your damn doctor? You got a concussion and you're kinda beat-up otherwise. But I don't think your arm's broken. You look like hell."

"Thanks, Vic." She managed a weak, watery smile.

"You want more detail than that, I gotta get the doc in here. Which I should do anyway." He stood up. "I got more important things to do than play nurse. Arrest reports to fill out."

"For who? Mickey's dead."

"His goons. One of them's right here along with the rest of this happy party, thanks to a tag-team effort by Corcoran and yours truly. Corcoran threw a knife at him, cut up his shoulder pretty bad, and I put a couple rounds in him, but I think he'll live. The other one's back at the Eightball in Holding. The Lieutenant's around somewhere, too. I'm telling you, this is a total shitshow and everybody's invited. I think you got some family on the way, come to think of it. Man, between us, we've pretty much filled up this hospital. We got you, your sister-in-law, that asshole I shot, the Patrolman who got nailed in Midtown, plus Thompson and Corcoran."

"How's Ian?" Erin struggled to swing her feet off the side of the bed. "Is he going to be okay?"

"How the hell do I know?" Vic said again, pushing her legs back into bed with surprising gentleness. "Look, you're not supposed to get up yet. Didn't you hear when I said you had a concussion? Those things screw with your balance. If you get up, you'll fall down and kill yourself and then the Lieutenant will yell at me."

Erin sagged back. But something else Vic had said struck her. "Corky's hurt? How?"

"Took one in the arm. But don't worry about him. Last I saw, he was flirting with the nurses. Speaking of which, I better get the doc now your brain's working. Be back in a minute." Vic left the room.

Chapter 15

The doctor arrived before Erin had quite decided to get up and go looking for her family on her own. It wasn't her brother, of course; they'd never let a doctor have his own sister for a patient. This doc was a gray-haired man with wire-rimmed glasses and a gentle smile.

"How are you feeling, Erin?" he asked.

"I'm fine," she said. "Just a headache."

"What's your name?" he asked.

She looked at him, surprised. "Erin. You just said that."

He smiled. "Humor me, please. Your full name?"

"Erin Catherine O'Reilly."

"Do you know how old you are?"

"Thirty-six."

"Do you know where you are?"

"Bellevue Hospital, Manhattan." She rolled her eyes. "New York City. USA. Planet Earth."

He nodded and made a couple of notes on his clipboard. "A man was in here with you. Do you remember him?"

"Yeah." She was getting impatient. "That's Vic Neshenko. I work with him."

"What work do you do?"

"I'm a police detective. Look, Doctor..."

"Nussbaum."

"Doctor Nussbaum, I know you've got your job to do, but so do I. I need to see Michelle O'Reilly as soon as possible. How long have I been here?"

"Do you know what day it is?"

"What day?" she echoed. "It's Tuesday. No, Wednesday. Wait..."

She couldn't remember. She hadn't been out for a full day, so she ought to know. But she didn't. What else might be missing? How did you know if you'd forgotten something? She sank back against her pillow and let out a shuddering breath.

"You've suffered a traumatic brain injury, Erin," Nussbaum said softly. "We're trying to determine what areas of your brain have been affected. Concussions aren't an exact science, I'm afraid, but I've worked with a number of cases like yours. I see no reason you won't make a full recovery, but you have to be patient."

"I haven't got time to be patient," she said. "I need to check on my family. I have a case to close."

"Surely you can let your coworkers carry some of the load. They understand your situation. Nobody's going to think any less of you."

"And my dog," she went on. "He's at the vet. He's hurt, too. I have to take care of him."

"Your family has been notified," Nussbaum said. "I've spoken with your brother. He's on staff here."

"I know that," she said sharply. "I don't care what that damn clipboard of yours says, my brain works just fine."

Nussbaum didn't get upset. He just nodded and made another note. "We'll want to keep you overnight for observation," he said. "Fortunately, your MRI showed no signs of intracranial bleeding, so I don't think surgery will be necessary. The brain swelling is going down on its own. You're a very lucky woman."

"I don't feel so lucky right now," she said bitterly. "What about the rest of me? Besides my head, I mean."

"Does anything else hurt?"

She considered. The pounding headache was drowning out most other sensations, but she was aware of a pain in her right upper arm. "Here," she said, patting her bicep and suppressing a wince. "Is it broken?" She'd forgotten Vic telling her about her arm only a few minutes earlier. If she'd remembered, it would have worried her even more.

"No, but it's badly bruised, and I think the bone may be bruised, too. It'll be sore for a while. Have you ever suffered a previous head injury?"

"Not that I remember. But then, how can I be sure?"

Nussbaum had the good grace to chuckle at that.

"I guess that's not the first time you've heard that one, huh?" she said.

"That's the good thing about amnesia jokes," he replied. "They're funny every time."

A man appeared in the doorway. "Can I come in?" he asked.

"She really shouldn't have more visitors right now," Nussbaum said without looking.

"Good thing I work here, then," Doctor Sean O'Reilly said, stepping into the room.

"Hey, Junior," Erin said.

"Hey, kiddo." Her oldest brother came to the bedside and took her hand in his. "How are you feeling?"

"Like I've been to an Irish wedding," she said. "You think my head's bad? You should see the other guy."

"Can you give us a minute, Ari?" Sean said to Nussbaum.

"All right. But she really should be resting." Nussbaum smiled at Erin and walked out of the room.

"I'm sorry," Erin said as soon as they were alone. "God, I'm so sorry. I—"

"Erin, you saved her," Sean said. He choked on a sudden sob and bent over her, gripping her hand tightly. "You found her and you fought for her and she's all right, she's safe. Thank you, thank you so much."

Erin had grown up with him and had never seen him lose his self-control so badly. It was the sheer relief of it, knowing Michelle was safe, after having to keep his shit together all day. She wasn't sure how to handle the situation. She awkwardly patted his shoulder.

"How did you find her?" he asked.

"I just followed my nose."

"How's that?"

"Mickey—the guy who took her—was wounded. I got a tipoff which led us to the guy who treated him. That guy remembered the way he smelled. It made me think of an old candy factory, which led us to the Domino Sugar Refinery."

"That big brick place in Brooklyn? That's where she was?"

"Yeah, that's the one. Have you seen Shelley?"

"Only for a couple minutes when they first brought her in. I've been taking care of Mr. Thompson. I'm going to hand them off in a couple hours. After that, they'll need six big guys and a crowbar to pry me away from Shelley."

"How's Ian?"

Sean smiled tightly and wiped at his eyes with his sleeve. "That's one tough young man," he said. "He sailed through the surgery. Not his first one, either, to judge from the scars on him. You know, I didn't recognize him at first. After a while in this job, you learn to just see the injuries. You don't even notice the faces. It's easier that way."

"What's his prognosis?" she asked.

"He took five bullets," he said, shaking his head. "The one in the arm was just a flesh wound and with the luck he had from the neck shot, he ought to buy some lotto tickets. It missed his carotid by about three millimeters, but tore through without hitting anything important. Then he took one in the right thigh which chipped the femur. That's a serious injury, but not life-threatening, and with proper rehab, he should regain full use of the limb. But he'll need crutches and it'll take months for full recovery."

"That's three," she said. "What about the others?"

"The other two were touchy," he said. "One clipped his lung. The bullet was still lodged in there. I had to go in and get it. But the operation was a success. The other took out a couple inches of intestine. Must've hurt like nobody's business, and there's always the risk of infection with abdominal wounds, but I resectioned the bowel and we pumped him full of antibiotics and fresh blood. I'm not too worried."

"Jesus," Erin said softly. "You're right. He's tough. He was still trying to reload when I got there. I think he was more annoyed at getting shot than anything."

"Officer Blake should make it, too," Sean went on. "Which is good, because we don't want the two dozen cops in our waiting room to burn down the hospital. He was only hit once, but it was right smack in the trachea. He almost drowned in his own blood. Ian didn't shoot him, did he?"

"Of course not! Ian would never shoot a cop!"

"Then why did the police shoot Ian?" Sean asked.

"What? I thought Mickey's guys shot him," Erin said.

Sean just shrugged. "That's a police question," he said. "I just stitch people back together. What do I know?"

"How long have I been here?" she asked suddenly. "What time is it?"

"Almost six o' clock," he said. "In the evening."

"Do I get something to eat?" she asked. "And I'm thirsty."

He reached across the bed and handed her a plastic water bottle. "I'm not surprised," he said. "They had you on a saline drip. That'll make you thirsty. I'm afraid you're on a liquid diet for today."

"That's not so bad," she said. "I don't know what they've got here, but if someone can make a run back to my place, they can grab a bottle of Glen D. That should do me just fine."

"Liquid, Erin. Not liquor. No booze for head cases."

She pouted. "I'm definitely leaving a bad review on Bellevue's website. I could really use a drink."

Sean was about to say something but was distracted by the arrival of a stout, motherly whirlwind. Mary O'Reilly was across the room before anyone could say or do anything, throwing her arms around Erin.

"Mom. Mom!" Erin exclaimed in a near-scream as Mary squeezed right on her bruised arm. The pain was sudden and excruciating.

"I'm sorry, dear," Mary said, letting go at once. "Your father and I got to town as soon as we could. He's got the grandchildren with him. But I just had to come here. You're so pale, dear. Almost green. I'll bet they aren't feeding you anything at all."

"Liquid diet, Mom," Sean said. "Doctor's orders."

"Well, you're a doctor," she said tartly. "You can write *new* doctor's orders."

He smiled. "I want her to get better, Mom. She'll be back on solids tomorrow. You can start stuffing food into her then."

"I didn't have time to bake anything," she said. "Your father hustled me out of the house so fast, I hardly had time to pack our overnight bag. But while he was getting his guns, I managed to grab a few things."

"He brought his guns?" Erin said, dismayed but not really surprised.

"Not all of them, dear. Just a couple of pistols and his hunting shotgun. He seemed to think the family was under attack or something. He drove very fast to get here. I thought we'd get pulled over for certain."

"So he's back at the Barley Corner?" Erin asked.

"That's right, dear. Your house is all covered with police tape, Junior."

"The upstairs should be all right," Erin said. "The kidnapping happened right at the front door. I don't think Mickey went more than a step or two inside. You'll be able to live there. CSU is probably already done processing the scene."

Doctor Nussbaum reappeared. "Every time I walk by, I see another visitor," he said sternly. "How did you get in here?"

Erin smothered a smile. She had yet to meet the man who could keep Mary away from one of her injured children.

"My patient has had a severe physical shock and needs her rest," Nussbaum went on. "I'm ordering everyone out of the room now. You'll be able to see her again soon."

"Don't worry, dear," Mary said, kissing Erin's cheek. "We're not going anywhere. There's a regular regiment of police officers just down the hall. I'll settle in with them. I brought some of my knitting."

*   *   *

Erin went from a slow burn to a boil. So she was hurt? Big deal. O'Reillys played through the pain. She should be checking on the others and figuring out who was responsible for the car bomb that had started this whole mess.

She thought of Rolf. He was just like her. As long as he was breathing, he'd want to be out doing his job. The only reason he was penned up at the vet was that he couldn't open doors. But she could.

She couldn't just make a run for the door. Her mom had told her a bunch of cops were hanging around the lobby, holding vigil for Officer Blake and, she supposed, her. And Mary would stop her before she made it halfway to the door. All that was assuming she was willing to charge off into the Manhattan streets wearing one of those absurd hospital gowns that didn't close in back, showing off her ass to every civilian in sight.

Erin saw a pile of clothes on a table. It looked like what she'd been wearing earlier. Maybe, if she stretched her arm just a little farther...

She couldn't quite reach. She cursed under her breath.

But she hadn't been specifically told not to stand up. Would she fall over? She didn't think so, but she hadn't had a concussion this bad before. Mickey sure did pack a mean right hook.

"The hell with it," Erin muttered. She wanted to reach her pants, specifically, and she meant to do it. She darted a quick look toward the door, making sure no nurses or doctors were passing. Then she swung her legs over the side of the bed and carefully stood up, holding onto the railing on the side of the bed just in case.

There was a moment of dizziness. Her headache got immediately worse as her heart forced more blood up into her skull. It was like a hammer pounding the inside of her head. She let the pain level off to a dull, sickening throb. Then she dared a step, and another. She didn't fall over. She put out a hand and picked up her clothes. Feeling very adventurous, she retreated back to the bed and sat down again to go through her pockets.

As she'd hoped, her phone was still in her hip pocket. She fished it out and checked it. Her heart sank. The screen was a crushed spider-web of cracks. She must have landed on it when she'd fallen over. She tried swiping it with her finger anyway.

The battered phone lit up, showing forty-seven percent charge and a helpful message indicating she'd missed some incoming calls. Erin blessed modern technology and checked the call history. She had sixteen calls, four from Lieutenant Webb, the other twelve from Carlyle's current burner phone.

"Mom and Dad must've talked to him by now," she said aloud. And she really needed to check in with Webb. But she owed it to Carlyle to at least let him know how she was. She hit the return call icon.

Carlyle picked up immediately. "Darling?" he asked, and though he would have sounded mostly calm to a stranger, she caught the anxious undertone.

"Yeah, it's me," she said. "Where are you?"

"I handed the wee ones off to your da a short while ago," he said. "I'm at the hospital now, with your mum."

"Then you know I'm okay," she said. "Why didn't you come with her to see me?"

"Don't you know, darling? This place is overrun with coppers. They're only letting in family, and even your mum had to fight for the privilege. Everyone's in a bit of an uproar. I really ought to be talking to Evan, sorting this shite out. I understand you took care of our little problem?"

"You could say that. I don't remember what happened, but Vic says I got him. Have you seen Ian?"

"I tried, but he's under guard. Apparently he's a person of interest, and the lads outside his door are distressingly incorruptible."

"Tell me you didn't try to bribe your way past a couple of NYPD officers," she said, finding it all too easy to imagine.

"I felt the lads out, but they weren't receptive," he said. "We really do need to be getting out ahead of this, but I've no intention of leaving you."

"You'd better go," she said, hating to say it but knowing it was true. "Talk to Evan. Make sure he understands, I only did it because he had Shelley. This wasn't an attack on him."

"Darling, don't you understand? You've done him a favor. This will only solidify our position. But it's best if he hears it from me, the sooner the better, you ken?"

"Yeah. I'll get in to see Ian as soon as I can, okay? I'll let you know how he is."

"That'd be grand, darling. If you're quite sure you're up for it?"

"Are you kidding? They can't keep me here, not for long. Did everything go okay with the kids? And my dad?"

"Aye, they're grand. We got on wonderfully well. Your da understands I've been trying to help."

"What about Corky?" she asked with a little more trepidation.

"Also under guard. I understand he's been arrested."

"Oh. Of course. I'll try to check on him, too."

"I love you, darling. And I thank the good Lord you're safe."

"I love you, too. And watch out when you talk to Evan."

"Erin, I've told you, he'll be pleased with what we've done."

"I'm not worried about him," she said. "Whoever planted that bomb on Mickey is still out there. They may make another try for you."

"Darling, no one's made a try for me but Mickey. And we agreed, the other lad wasn't even trying to kill him."

"I know what I'm talking about," Erin said. "They set Mickey up to come after us... after you. He missed, so maybe they'll try again. And Ian can't watch your back right now."

"Point well taken, darling. I'll be cautious. Will you be reachable at this number?"

"I think so."

"Then I'll ring you later this evening."

"Thanks."

"Slán agat, darling."

"Bye," she said, not knowing the Irish words but making an educated guess.

Then she called her boss. Webb took a little longer to answer, maybe because he wasn't as worried about her, or maybe because he was busy. She thought it would roll to voicemail, but he picked up just after the fourth ring.

"So you're still with us," he said.

"Yes, sir. Back on duty."

"Like hell you are. You're on medical leave."

"Pretty sure I'm not, sir."

"Are you in a hospital bed right now?"

"Yes, sir."

"Have you been cleared for duty by your physician?"

She sighed. "Not yet, sir."

"So if you're not on medical leave, what exactly would you call it?"

"Down but not out, sir."

"I like your spirit, but I don't want you keeling over. Then you'd sue the department and I'd lose my pension."

"I would never. I hate lawyers."

"How are you feeling, O'Reilly?"

"You should see the other guy," she said for the second time that day.

"I heard from Neshenko that you performed a little open-head surgery. Have you filed your use-of-force report yet?"

"Like you said, sir, I'm on leave. Haven't done any paperwork."

"Which reminds me, if you're not on medical leave, you're on admin leave because you shot a guy."

"Oh. Yeah."

"I'll tell the Captain what's going on. He'll have someone on the way to take your statement. It should be pretty routine, but until you've done it, we can't discuss the incident. Neshenko also told me he recovered your sister-in-law. He's talking to her right now."

"Really?"

"Yeah, he said he was at the hospital anyway, and she was right down the hall. Apparently he's been a little worried about you."

"He shouldn't be. I've got a hard head."

He chuckled dryly. "So I've learned. I can tell you we've got two of Connor's guys, one seriously injured, the other intact. I took a run at the healthy one, but he lawyered up. He's a two-time loser name of Cole Phillips. You know him?"

"No. I don't hang around Mickey's guys." She didn't bother to add that they were mostly violent psychopaths. Webb knew that already.

"Well, we've got him cold on kidnapping, and he's at least an accomplice for the shooting of two of ours, so he's going away for a long time. You hear about Blake and Washburn?"

"Washburn's the one who didn't make it?" she asked.

"Yeah. CSU's preliminary report is that both of them were shot by a MAC-10, probably the same one Neshenko recovered at the Domino Refinery from the guy he tagged. You didn't see that part of the incident?"

"No, sir. I was in the other room. Vic and Corky—James Corcoran, I mean—sorted that out."

"Did the two of you deputize him, or what?"

"No, he was there as a free agent."

It was Webb's turn to sigh. "I see. You do understand he's under arrest, right?"

"Yes, sir."

"We'll sort him out later."

"Yes, sir."

"If we can."

"Yes, sir."

"Anyway, our officers were hit by .45-caliber slugs. Your boy Thompson was armed with a nine-millimeter, so it appears he didn't shoot any cops."

"I know he didn't. Why does everyone seem to think he did?"

"Maybe because he's a hardened combat veteran who's killed multiple people and who was involved in a three-way gunfight in the middle of Manhattan. Regardless, I've taken a look at the dashcam footage from the squad car. It pretty clearly shows Thompson engaging the guys across the street. We've got him on camera pumping bullets into a vehicle, almost certainly killing both the guys we found in that SUV."

"They were kidnapping my sister-in-law," she said. "He was trying to stop them."

"I know, O'Reilly. I know. I'm just telling you what the video shows. The car pulls up, the officers jump out, ID themselves, and order Thompson to drop the gun. He keeps shooting. So they open fire."

Erin closed her eyes. A wave of nausea hit her, maybe from the concussion, maybe from what Webb was saying. "So Ian didn't get shot by Mickey or his guys," she said. "He was shot by the police. He was just trying to help and we damn near killed him."

"The officers didn't know," Webb said tiredly. "All they saw was a gangland shootout."

"He loves my brother's family," she said. "They took him in. The kids... the kids think he's great. He's eaten at their table." Suddenly, she was trying not to cry, not to completely lose it while talking to her commanding officer.

Webb heard the hitch in her voice. "IAB should be there soon," he said, making his own voice brisk and businesslike. "It'll probably be Lieutenant Keane, sad to say. Take a minute, think over what happened. You'll be fine. Connor was a dangerous man, a known killer. Just tell the truth, keep it simple, and answer his questions."

"Thanks, sir."

"I'm tied up with all kinds of red tape here, but I'll come by the hospital in a couple of hours. Will you still be there?"

"Just where would I be going, sir?"

"I don't know, O'Reilly. I never know what you're up to. Get better. We're shorthanded enough as it is."

"You're all heart, sir."

Chapter 16

Erin had been joking with Webb, but compared to Lieutenant Keane, Webb was a bleeding-heart softie. Keane was the youngest Lieutenant in the NYPD, a sharp-faced, sharp-witted son of a bitch who'd climbed the departmental ladder on a combination of smarts, ambition, and ruthlessness. His nickname was "The Bloodhound," which Erin thought was an insult to dogs.

She was grateful for Webb's advance warning. When Keane walked into her room carrying a black briefcase and clad in a perfectly-ironed black suit, she was as ready for him as she could be. She just wished she'd had time to put on her street clothes after hanging up with Webb. When talking to the head of the Eightball's Internal Affairs Bureau, she needed every edge she could get, and worrying about her hospital gown falling off put her at a disadvantage.

She was surprised, however, at Keane's companion. Captain Holliday had come with the IAB officer. That was probably a good thing. Holliday took care of his people and would have her back. But the Captain's face, screened by his Wild West gunslinger's mustache, was impossible to read.

"Good evening, Detective," Keane said, offering his hand. She leaned forward, shook briefly, and let go. She didn't like to touch Keane more than absolutely necessary.

"How are you holding up, Detective?" Holliday asked.

"I'm fine, sir," she said. "I'll be back on duty as soon as I'm cleared."

"If you'd get the door, please, Captain?" Keane said.

Holliday nodded and closed the door. Keane laid his briefcase on the table, popped the catches, opened it, and took out an old-style tape recorder. Erin found it quaint, but didn't let down her guard. She neither liked nor trusted Keane.

"If you're not feeling up for this, we can postpone," Keane said.

"I said I'm fine," she said, straightening her shoulders. She wished her hair wasn't such a tangled mess. She probably looked terrible. Why did Keane always have to be so damned put-together? He probably had his dry-cleaner on speed dial.

"You have the right to request an attorney from the Union," Keane said.

"I don't want a damn lawyer," Erin said. That was probably stupid of her. Every cop knew that if you got arrested, whether you were innocent or not, the first word out of your mouth should be "lawyer." But she just wanted to get the whole thing over with.

Keane nodded and sat down. Holliday remained standing a little behind the Lieutenant on one side, hands clasped behind his back.

Keane pressed a button on the recorder. "First interview with Detective Second Grade Erin O'Reilly subsequent to fatal shooting of Michael Connor. Location is Bellevue Hospital. Interview is being conducted by Lieutenant Andrew Keane, witnessed by Captain Fenton Holliday, Precinct 8 Commanding Officer. Let the record show, subject has waived her right to legal representation. Detective O'Reilly, this interview is being recorded. Do you understand the preceding?"

"Yes," Erin said.

"For what reason did you enter the Domino Sugar Refinery?"

"We'd received a tip that Mickey Connor might be there."

"Where did this tip originate?"

"Confidential informant with connections to the O'Malley criminal organization."

"Who accompanied you?"

"Detective Third Grade Vic Neshenko and my K-9 Rolf."

"Did you obtain a search warrant prior to entering the refinery?"

"No."

"Why not?"

"There wasn't time. Mickey had abducted a woman and we believed her life was in imminent danger."

"What is your relationship to the alleged kidnapping victim?"

"She's my sister-in-law, Michelle O'Reilly."

"Did you call for backup?"

"Yes. Vic made the call."

"According to the call to Dispatch, Detective Neshenko reported a 10-13 with shots fired," Keane said. "That suggests the incident was already in progress when he called for backup. Is that correct?"

"Yes," Erin said. Of course Keane had already listened to the recorded call. He didn't miss a single detail.

"Why didn't you call for backup earlier?"

"We had no firm evidence Mickey was there."

"But your evidence was firm enough to make an illegal entry?" Keane asked, raising an eyebrow.

Holliday shifted and his mustache twitched. He shot Erin a look that clearly told her to choose her next words very carefully.

"We had probable cause of a crime in progress," Erin said.

"What probable cause?" Keane asked.

"I recognized a vehicle parked outside. It was a yellow BMW convertible owned by James Corcoran. He's an O'Malley associate."

"Is he connected with Michael Connor?"

"No. Their relationship was antagonistic."

"What was Corcoran doing there?"

"I believe he was attempting to rescue Shelley... the kidnapping victim. I anticipated violence between him and Mickey, so I made entry. Vic suggested hanging back and calling for backup. I overruled him. It was my responsibility as ranking officer."

Keane nodded. "What happened then?"

Erin wondered how much she could trust her recollections. Her head was still pounding and her thoughts were a little muddled. "We had a sample of Mickey's blood. I gave it to Rolf and put him on the scent. We followed him into the factory. Then we heard gunfire. One shooter, maybe two. At that time, Vic called it in."

"But you didn't wait for other officers to arrive?"

"I believed the victim's life was in immediate danger."

"So you charged in," Keane said.

"We found Corky engaged in a standoff with two shooters," she said.

"Was Corcoran exchanging fire with these subjects?" Keane asked.

"Corky doesn't carry a gun," she said. "Vic told me Corky threw a knife at one of them and wounded him."

"A knife was recovered from one of the subjects," Holliday confirmed. "It was lodged in his right shoulder between the collarbone and the scapula."

"Vic engaged the shooters," Erin went on. "I followed Rolf into the next room."

"You didn't stay to assist Detective Neshenko?" Keane asked.

"He had it under control," she said. "I had to find Mickey and Shelley, and Rolf was on Mickey's scent. We found him in the locker room."

"How did the incident unfold?"

"He kicked Rolf across the room and charged me. I shot him a couple of times center mass, but he didn't stop." She paused. It was hard to remember. Everything had been so fast. She concentrated on her body's various aches, retracing the action by way of remembered pain. "He hit me just under the shoulder and I lost my grip on my sidearm. Then he hit me again, on the side of the head. I'm not a hundred percent clear on what happened after that. Rolf jumped him and bit him. He... beat Rolf against a locker a few times. I think he knocked my K-9 out. Then he grabbed me."

"He didn't punch you again?" Keane asked.

"No. I don't think his right arm was working properly. Rolf bit him pretty hard. I wouldn't be surprised if that arm was broken. He picked me up with his left hand."

"When you say he picked you up, what do you mean?"

"He lifted me off the ground. Into the air. I went for my backup piece and I guess I shot him."

Keane frowned. "You guess?"

"I don't remember the shot. The next thing I remember is being here, throwing up into a wastebasket." She shrugged. Her right arm told her shrugging had been a bad idea. "That's what happened."

"Was Mr. Connor armed when you shot him?" Keane asked.

She gave him an incredulous look. "Have you ever seen Mickey Connor?"

"The man was a heavyweight boxer," Holliday said quietly. "He was very large and physically intimidating."

"I'm aware of Mr. Connor's history and appearance," Keane said. "Please answer the question, Detective."

"He had twenty dollars in his hands," she said. "A roll of quarters in each fist. That's it, and it was plenty. He damn near killed Rolf and me both."

"Did you identify yourself prior to firing?"

"He was looking right at me."

"But you did not identify yourself as a police officer?" he pressed.

"I was wearing a vest that said POLICE in big white letters," she snapped. "Mickey knew me on sight. This isn't the first time I've tangled with him, it was just the last. We've been up close, eyeball to eyeball. It isn't even the first time he's tried to kill me."

"Really?" Keane's eyebrow went up again. "Why didn't you arrest him then?"

"You know why."

"Ah." Keane gave Holliday a significant look. As far as Erin knew, they were the only high-ranking officers at the Eightball who were aware of her undercover work.

"It's in Phil's file... Lieutenant Stachowski, I mean. I reported the incident to him."

"Did you make any effort to detain Mr. Connor without lethal force?" Keane asked.

"I didn't have the chance. He wasn't going to come quietly."

"So you shot an unarmed criminal, with whom you had a prior history, without warning?" Keane asked quietly. "While in the course of a warrantless search?"

"Lieutenant," Holliday said softly. He covered it well, but Erin could tell he was very angry at Keane.

"I shot a murderous thug who'd kidnapped a woman and, together with his goons, killed one police officer and critically injured another," Erin retorted, her temper getting the better of her. "I put down a man who was trying to kill me and my K-9, and who nearly succeeded. You're damn lucky I'm able to give you this statement. I'm in the friggin' hospital, sir, with my brain scrambled, and you want to talk about being unarmed? That son of a bitch had to go down. Are you asking me if I had to do it? Of course I did. Are you asking if I'd do it again? Hell yes, I would. Every time. So cut the bullshit. With all due respect, sir."

Keane listened to her outburst, tapping the tips of his index fingers together. When she ran out of breath, he smiled. It wasn't a pleasant expression.

"I see," he said. "I think that concludes the interview. Thank you for your candor, Detective O'Reilly." He pushed the button on the recorder again, stopping the tape. He stood up.

"That's it?" Erin asked. "What now?"

"That's it," Keane said. "And while we're off the record, well done, Detective. I don't think you have anything to worry about. This isn't your first lethal force incident, and that is some cause for concern, but frankly, no one in New York is going to lose any sleep over a man like Connor being shot. He was, as you say, a murderous thug."

"Then what was the point of all that?" she demanded.

"Procedure, Detective," Holliday said. "We have rules for a reason. You know that."

"You didn't need to come all the way here, sir," she said to him. "Lieutenant Keane could've done it himself."

"I wanted to talk with you about how this will affect the other matter," Holliday said. "We need to discuss your ongoing special assignment."

"Yes, sir."

"As of this moment, your undercover operation is terminated."

"You can't do that!" Erin burst out.

Holliday's eyes went cold. "I'm the commanding officer of Precinct 8, Detective," he said. "The safety of its officers, and of New York's population, is my responsibility. I can do that, and I've just done it. I'll contact Lieutenant Stachowski. He'll handle bringing you in."

"We're not ready!" she protested.

"Then we'll get as many of them as we can," the Captain said. "Your family was placed in direct jeopardy, Detective. There's no walking that back."

"Captain," Keane said. "Perhaps we should think on this before taking any rash action."

"Rash?" Holliday echoed, turning on him. "You're saying we should wait for more civilians to get hurt? What about our officers? We've got two in the hospital and one in the morgue because of this."

Erin flinched. That was a weight she'd have to carry. "We can't let that be for nothing," she said.

"Detective O'Reilly is right," Keane said. "We can still salvage this. I can't condone the operation being concluded at this juncture."

"This operation isn't under IAB jurisdiction," Holliday snapped. "I say when it's over, *Lieutenant*."

Keane's jaw tightened, the most visible display of anger Erin had ever seen on his face. She saw a sharp response flicker in his eyes. But he only said, "I'll update the file accordingly, *Captain*."

"I'm sorry, O'Reilly," Holliday said more gently. "But this is life and death."

"Yes, sir," she said, knowing it was hopeless but needing to try. "It is. And that's why we don't have a choice—"

The door opened. Holliday spun on his heel, then relaxed when a nurse entered the room with a tray in her hands.

"Suppertime," the nurse said.

"We'll leave you to it," Holliday said. "We're done here. And good work, Detective." He smiled sadly.

Erin's stomach growled. Her nausea was gone and her belly was empty. Then she saw what was on the tray: a bowl of beef broth, a glass of clear juice, a juice box, and a bowl of lime Jell-O.

"Liquid diet," she sighed. On top of everything else. She knew it was what the doctors thought she needed, but right then, she might have considered killing someone else if it would've gotten her a bowl of the Barley Corner's Irish stew. Her life was falling apart. The least they could do was give her some decent comfort food.

* * *

Erin gave it fifteen endless minutes, some of the longest of her life, making sure Keane and Holliday had time to leave. Then she got dressed and got the hell out of there.

She wasn't a prisoner. And a doctor's instructions were just advice. They told people not to smoke, they told them to lose weight. And that might be good advice, but look at all the overweight, nicotine-addicted doctors in the world. So she still had a headache? Big deal. She felt okay, more or less. And if they hadn't expected her to get up, they shouldn't have left her clothes.

Just putting on pants and a shirt, even if they smelled like rust and burnt sugar, made her feel better. Her holsters were there too, but of course the guns had been tagged and bagged as evidence. At least they'd left her gold shield, which she clipped to her belt. Her room had a tiny half-bathroom with a sink and a mirror. She did what she could with her hair, which wasn't much, and tied it back in a scraggly ponytail. Then she splashed water on her face, took a deep breath, and stepped out into the hallway.

It was deserted except for a uniformed officer in a chair by the elevators. He was reading a paperback thriller, some trashy cop novel by some guy she'd never heard of. He looked bored out of his skull. She walked up to him and cleared her throat.

"Help you, ma'am?" he asked, setting down the book. "This is a restricted area."

She tapped her gold shield.

"Oh, right," he said, straightening his spine. "Sorry, Detective."

"I'm looking for Michelle O'Reilly," she said. "Has she been released yet?"

"She's that tall, dark-haired lady they brought in this afternoon?"

"Yeah."

"Nope. One of your people went in to talk to her a while back."

"Detective Neshenko? Big blond guy with a crooked nose?"

"That's him."

"He still here?"

"No, he left with that Captain, the one with the mustache, and the other guy. The one who looks like a weasel."

"You're not from the Eightball, are you," Erin said. Any Patrol cop from Precinct 8 would have recognized Keane and would have known better than to describe him that way.

"No, ma'am. You're on the One Three's turf."

"I knew that." She did know that. Why hadn't she remembered it? Her head throbbed. "Which room is Ms. O'Reilly in?" she asked.

"Third one on the left." He pointed.

"Thanks." Erin left him to his paperback and went to the indicated room. The door was closed, which was a little unusual. Doctors and nurses liked open doors in hospitals, so they could hear anything untoward. But Michelle was under police protection and she'd just been rescued. They'd probably bent the rules for her.

Erin knocked lightly, paused a moment, and opened the door. "Shelley?" she called softly, poking her head around the door.

The room looked just like Erin's, a standard, antiseptic hospital recovery room. Michelle was sitting on the edge of the bed. Sean O'Reilly Junior was a few feet away, facing the window, his arms crossed. Erin couldn't see his face. Michelle's was flushed and puffy. The woman's eyes were bloodshot and wet streaks ran down her cheeks. She'd obviously been crying.

"You're supposed to be in bed," Erin's brother said without turning. Erin blinked at the sound of his voice. He'd been upset earlier, and scared, but this was different. Now he sounded lifeless, numb.

"I needed to talk to Shelley," she said. "Hey, sis. I haven't seen you yet. How are you doing?"

"She already gave her statement to your colleague," Sean said, still in that flat, dead voice. "There's nothing more to say."

"What's going on here?" Erin asked, stepping farther into the room. "Sean? Shelley?"

"Thanks for rescuing me, Erin," Michelle said. She was hoarse, and looked very tired, but Erin couldn't see any visible injuries. That was a relief.

"Shelley, what happened?"

"Why don't you ask that other detective?" Sean suggested.

"Hey, Junior," Erin said. "If you want to contribute to the conversation, why don't you look at me while you do it?"

Sean turned around and Erin wished he hadn't. His face looked absolutely terrible. None of Erin's brothers were wimps. Crying hadn't been a big part of their upbringing. She'd never seen him with such a haunted, hurt look in his eyes. Most of what she saw was pain, but under it was a seething anger, a rage Sean O'Reilly Junior had never shown the world. He was a doctor, a man who'd devoted his life to putting broken people back together. He was strong, but gentle. Not tonight.

Erin took an involuntary half-step backward. "What happened?" she asked again.

"I told him," Michelle whispered. "Everything."

"Did Mickey... do anything to you?" Erin asked.

Michelle shook her head. "Not like that. But he... he told me things. What he was going to do. He said he was looking forward to it. That... man was... he was... I've never been so scared."

"I don't blame you," Erin agreed. "I don't know if I've ever met a scarier guy. How did things go down?"

"The doorbell rang," Michelle said. "I looked out the front window and saw... the biggest man I've ever seen in my life. Another guy was with him. I didn't like the look of them. I opened the door a crack, to see what they wanted, but I kept it on the chain. I thought... I don't know, maybe they were lost, or they were delivery people or something. It was stupid. I shouldn't have opened the door."

"It wouldn't have mattered," Erin said grimly. "I don't think your front door would've kept him out."

"I know," Michelle said quietly. "He kicked the door and the chain broke and the door just splintered. The door hit me and I fell over. Then he bent over and picked me up. It was easy for him. He just scooped me up like I was a doll or something, and he brought his face up close to mine and..." She shuddered.

"What did he do?" Erin asked.

"He asked where my kids were," Michelle said.

"God," Erin whispered.

"I didn't want to tell him. He said he'd hurt me if I didn't call them. I... I didn't want to. But I was so scared. I didn't know what to do."

"Anna didn't hear you," Erin said.

"No," Michelle said. "Right then I heard a man shout, 'Look out, ma'am! Get down!' And the shooting started. I think... I'm pretty sure it was Ian shouting."

"It was," Erin said. "He was following Mickey, keeping an eye on him. He wasn't supposed to get involved, but when he saw what Mickey was doing, I guess he felt like he had to do something."

"Then there was a crash," Michelle went on. "A couple of cars ran into each other on the street. Then the big man's friend said, 'Mick, we've gotta go!' The big guy didn't want to, but then he grunted and I saw his arm start bleeding. I guess he'd just been shot. So he carried me down the steps, holding me in front of him."

"A human shield," Erin said. So that was how Mickey had gotten away. Otherwise Ian would've mowed him down. She was surprised he'd tried even the one shot on Mickey while Michelle had been so close to him. But then again, Ian was an exceptional marksman.

"There was more shooting," Michelle went on. "And shouting. I think it was the police; I heard a siren. The other man, the one next to the big one, pulled out his gun and shot at them. I saw Ian, just for a second. He was... he was crossing the street toward us. There was blood all over him, but he kept coming, pointing a gun at us, but it didn't fire. I think maybe..."

"The gun was empty," Erin said. "He was out of ammo."

"That makes sense," Michelle said. "Then he fell down, in the street, and didn't get up. I screamed and the big man squeezed my neck. He said if I didn't shut up he'd break it. And he carried me down the street, around the corner. The other guy was still with us. They flagged down a taxi. When it stopped, the big guy broke the window with his fist and pulled the driver right out the window into the street."

"Did he put you down to do that?" Erin asked.

"No. He did it with one hand. The injured one. I couldn't believe how strong he was. He hit the driver and threw him onto the sidewalk. Then his friend got in the driver's seat and he got in back with me. We drove for a while. He told me to keep my mouth shut or he'd kill me. I don't think... I don't think he was kidding."

"He wasn't," Erin said. "You did the right thing."

Michelle swallowed. "We drove to a clinic and parked near it. The big guy went in, but the other one stayed with me, pointing his gun at me. I thought maybe I should run, or try to disarm him. It looks so easy when they do it in the movies."

"It's harder than it looks," Erin said. "If you'd tried, he would've shot you."

"I couldn't, anyway," Michelle said miserably. "I was too scared. I kept thinking I was going to die, and I didn't want to. I just froze. I couldn't do anything."

"What happened after that?"

"He came out again. His arm was stitched up and he had a bottle of pills and a bag of powder. He took a handful of the pills and snorted the powder up his nose. I think it must have been cocaine. And we drove south to Long Island. We went into a big, old brick building. The other guy drove the car away. I don't know what happened to him. The big guy put me in an office and... and he..."

Michelle stopped. Her eyes filled with tears. Sean, to Erin's surprise, didn't put out a hand or make any move toward her. He just stood there with that ravaged, haunted look on his face, saying nothing. Erin laid her own hand on her sister-in-law's shoulder.

"It's okay, Shelley," she said. "He can't hurt you. He's gone."

"He told me to... to take off my shirt. He said if I didn't, he'd do it himself and make it hurt. So I did. I thought... I thought maybe, if I did what he wanted, he'd let me go. I just wanted to see my children again. I'd do anything he told me to."

"You said he didn't do anything," Erin said.

"No. He just looked and... and smiled. I think he just liked seeing me scared. He... he tied me to an old chair, my wrists and my legs. And he started asking me things. About you."

"Me?" Erin said, surprised.

Michelle nodded. "He wanted to know where you liked to go, what your schedule was, everything like that. And he wanted to know about your brothers, their families, everything."

Erin finally understood. "He was planning to get to me," she said.

"I told him the truth," Michelle said in a low voice. "He said if I lied he'd... do things to me. I felt so helpless. I kept begging him to let me go. He liked hearing me beg and... and cry. I think... I think it got him... you know. He liked it."

"Yeah, I know," Erin said through clenched teeth. If Mickey had been in that room at that moment, and if she'd had her guns, she would gladly have shot him again.

"He had another guy with him," Michelle continued. "I think he was waiting for him where we were. He was... looking at me. And saying things. Nasty things. But the big guy made him leave. He told him to keep an eye out for company. Then, a while later, there was some shooting and I heard shouting. He tied a rag around my mouth and left me there. I tried to get free. I thought if maybe I could get my hands loose, I could get away. But the knots were too tight. Then I heard more shooting and I thought I heard Rolf growling."

"Yeah, that was us," Erin said.

"Then Detective Neshenko came in. I was scared of him until I saw the POLICE label on his chest. He... he untied me and took off his shirt and put it on me. So I was covered up. And then he took me out to the ambulance. A lot of other police were there, too, and you were in the ambulance."

God bless Vic, Erin thought. So that was why he hadn't had his shirt at the hospital. "Was I still out cold?" she asked.

"No, you were awake, but you were saying strange things, things that didn't make any sense," Michelle said. "The paramedics were worried about you. They put on the siren and drove to the hospital really fast. Detective Neshenko stayed behind, to take care of Rolf, but he said he'd catch up. And we ended up here."

"Shelley," Erin said. "You've got nothing to be ashamed of."

Sean barked a single harsh syllable that was almost too bitter to be laughter.

Erin turned on her brother. "What the hell is the matter with you?" she snapped. "This is your wife! The mother of your kids! And she's the kindest, sweetest person I know! She's been afraid for her life. Do you have any idea what kind of people those were who grabbed her? Because I do! So why don't you show some basic goddamn decency?"

"Erin, don't," Michelle said. "It's not his fault."

"Well it's sure as hell not yours, either!" Erin wasn't about to let him get away with blaming the victim. "You think I'm too beat-up to kick your ass, Junior? Because I'll be glad to!"

"Erin," Michelle said again. "I told him. About..."

"Am I interrupting something?" a familiar Irish brogue inquired from the direction of the doorway.

All three heads turned to James Corcoran. He had his arm in a sling and he looked pale. He was smiling, but it looked more uncertain than usual.

"That's him, isn't it," Sean said softly.

Michelle's eyes gave him all the answer he needed.

"What's *he* doing here?" Sean asked. He started toward the door, hands clenching into fists.

"Hey, Junior, take it easy," Erin said, not liking the look in his eye.

"I needed to see her," Corky said, nodding toward Michelle. "And to apologize for her troubles. It's at least partly on my account that she's had these difficulties, so I wanted to make what amends I could."

"You slick son of a bitch," Sean said in a low, deadly voice. "You come in here? To see *my wife?*"

Erin saw her brother's hands come up, saw him start swinging. If she'd been a little quicker, she could have stopped him, but she'd never expected her kindhearted big brother to physically attack a patient in his own hospital. Even now, watching it happen, she was having trouble believing it.

Sean was no boxer. It was a clumsy, amateurish swing. Corky was fast, with better reflexes than anyone Erin knew. Even injured, he should have been able to dodge. He saw the fist coming a mile off, with plenty of time to block or duck out of the way.

He just stood there and let it happen. As Sean's fist connected, Erin saw the look in Corky's eyes. He felt he deserved it, maybe even wanted it to happen.

The punch might have been bad technique, but Sean was bigger than Corky and kept himself in decent shape. And he'd swung like he meant it. The blow caught Corky squarely on the side of the face, just over the jaw. The smaller man was hurled sideways, bouncing off the wall. Corky reeled but didn't go down. He stayed standing, making no move to defend himself or to retaliate. Sean wound up for another swing.

"Hey! Knock it off!"

The Patrol officer from the hallway had followed Corky into Michelle's room, apparently suspicious of his intentions, but a little late arriving. Now, finding a patient getting pummeled by a doctor, the cop didn't know quite what to do, so tried just shouting.

It worked long enough for Erin to recover her wits and throw an arm around her brother, pulling him away from his target. The uniform grabbed Corky, which was unnecessary. The Irishman was completely passive and cooperative.

"Hey, Junior!" Erin shouted in his face. "Snap out of it! Come on! This isn't you!"

Sean's face was twisted into an angry snarl. "Get him out of here!" he growled at the cop. "Or I'm going to kill him!"

"He's a patient!" Erin said, giving him a shake. "You're a doctor! Think!"

She saw a glimmer of sanity return to Sean's eyes. He stopped struggling. She nodded to the cop.

"Better get him back to his room," she said.

"Jesus Christ," the uniform said. "I thought I was supposed to protect you guys from people out there, not in here! Is he gonna press charges, you think?"

"No one's pressing anything," Erin said. "Go!"

The patrolman shepherded Corky out of the room. Erin kept holding her brother. He sagged against her. To her mixed shock and relief, she felt his shoulders shake and he began sobbing into her. She looked around him at Michelle, who was staring wide-eyed at them. Erin nodded to her. Michelle took the cue, stood up, and cautiously approached her husband. She hesitantly touched his back.

Erin disengaged from Sean, steering him into his wife's arms. This was something they'd need to work out for themselves. She lingered a moment to make sure there wouldn't be any more violence. There was nothing more she could do. She backed out of the room, closing the door behind her.

Chapter 17

Erin wanted, needed to get out of the hospital. Every door she opened, every person she talked to, only led to more pain. How could her brother stand it? It was a wonder he hadn't cracked long before. But to see him actually hit another man... she could still hardly believe it.

She had to see Carlyle, to make sure everything was sorted out with the O'Malleys. She had to focus on work, because every time she tried to think of anything else, it hurt.

"Prioritize," she said to herself.

"You okay, Detective?" the Patrol cop from Precinct 13 asked.

"Yeah," she said. "What were you doing, letting Corcoran into another patient's room like that?"

"Sorry," he said. "My job's to make sure nobody unauthorized comes onto this floor. Nobody said nothin' about patients and staff. You were there, too. Why didn't you stop them?"

She shook her head. That required more of an answer than she was ready to give. "Where's Ian Thompson?" she asked. She couldn't go to Carlyle until she'd seen Ian. That was the last piece of business she meant to conduct in this God-awful place.

"End of the hall," he said. "Careful. They said he was in pretty rough shape."

"Thanks."

The hallway seemed very long. Her shoes squeaked plaintively on the polished floor. A wave of dizziness washed over her. She leaned against the wall, bracing herself with her hand until her head cleared. She knew damn well she ought to go back to bed. But she kept walking.

The rhythmic beeping of life-support machines greeted her like some alien species trying to make contact. She didn't know what any of the sounds meant, but took comfort from their repetitive pattern. If Ian was getting worse, alarms would probably be going off. She knew she wasn't going to like what she saw, but she couldn't turn back now. She steeled herself and stepped inside.

It wasn't as bad as she'd feared. The room was nearly dark, lit only by a faint night-light. Ian lay with his eyes closed, asleep or unconscious. He'd been intubated, so a plastic hose was taped to his mouth. Another, thinner hose was plugged into his nostrils. His neck had a clean white bandage wrapped around it. More bandages swathed his left bicep. The rest of his wounds were hidden under his blanket. His chest rose and fell. He was breathing on his own. If he'd been hit in the lung, like her brother had said, being able to breathe without a machine was excellent news.

"Thanks," she said softly, not knowing if he could hear her or not. "For Shelley. And Anna and Patrick. I'm sorry."

Ian's face was calm, no hint of pain in it. That was something to be thankful for. There'd be plenty of time for hurting.

*   *   *

Getting out of the hospital was annoying, but not difficult. Erin's patient record got marked "AMA," which meant she was getting discharged "Against Medical Advice," which in turn meant she couldn't sue Bellevue if she fell over dead once she stepped out the doors. The one stumbling block she was worried about was dealing with her brother, but she didn't see Sean anywhere. Either he'd gone back to work, or else he was still with Michelle, working through their relationship issues.

When she signed out and walked into the lobby, she was greeted by two dozen cheering NYPD officers. The room was full of cops, all of them grinning and applauding. She ran a gauntlet of handshakes, backslaps, and smiling faces. She recognized several faces from the Eightball. There were Polikowski and Worth, Patrol cops who'd helped her on a stakeout. There was Sergeant Brown from Vice, with the only smile she'd ever seen on his scarred, cynical face. And there, next to Mary O'Reilly, was Sergeant Malcolm, her dad's old friend, with honest to God tears in his eyes.

Erin hoped she wasn't getting too misty herself. She eased through the crowd toward the exit. Her mom intercepted her ten feet short of her goal and wrapped her in a motherly hug. That drew the expected chorus of "Awww," from the assembled officers.

"I need a car, Mom," Erin said.

"Why don't you just hijack an ambulance?" Malcolm suggested.

"With all these cops around? I don't think so." She turned to her mom. "Where's Carlyle?"

"He said he had urgent business, dear," Mary said. "Something about his boss. I thought he owned his own pub. What boss was he talking about?"

"Where did he go?"

"I don't know, honey. You look a little pale. Should you really be up and around?"

"I'm fine," Erin lied automatically. "How about Rolf?"

"He's at the emergency veterinary clinic," Mary said.

"I know the place," Malcolm said. As Desk Sergeant at the Eightball, he had access to all the officers' emergency contacts, including Rolf's 24-hour vet. "I can get you there. My car's outside."

"Aren't you supposed to be on duty?" Erin asked.

"I got off at five," he said. "Came straight over. You think I'm going to abandon Sean O'Reilly's kid? I'll get you to your dog, then I'll take you and your mom wherever you need to go."

"Thanks," she said. "First the vet, then the Barley Corner."

It was only a few minutes' drive to the vet, where Erin found a tired-looking assistant. The young woman took her back to a kennel. There was Rolf, pacing along the front wall and panting. When he saw Erin, the Shepherd stopped. He cocked his head at her and wagged his tail. A low whine emanated from his mouth.

Erin opened the gate and dropped to one knee. "Hey there, kiddo," she said. The dog thrust his muzzle against her shoulder and leaned into her, his tail wagging harder.

"Be careful with him," the tech advised. "He's suffered a significant concussion and three cracked ribs. He didn't need any stitches, so he doesn't have to wear a cone, but he's got to take it easy. I can give you some pills for the pain."

Erin drew back and looked her partner over. Rolf stared back, denying he was in any pain whatsoever. If there were more bad guys to bite, he was volunteering to jump right back into action.

"Easy, tough guy," she murmured. "Plenty of time for that later."

"Are you crying, dear?" Mary asked when Erin led Rolf past the front desk.

"Of course not," Erin lied. "He saved my life, you know, Mom."

"He's a good boy," Mary said, beaming at Rolf. The look in her eyes promised many, many treats in Rolf's future.

"The best," Erin agreed.

On the way to the Barley Corner, Mary rode shotgun in Malcolm's Crown Victoria, so Erin could stay in back with Rolf. Despite the Shepherd's stoicism, he was obviously hurting. He kept panting and didn't want to lie down on his injured ribs. All Erin could do was gently rub his ears and murmur *"zei brav"* over and over to him.

Rolf didn't understand what all the fuss was about. He knew he was a good boy. He was a little disappointed he'd lost his grip on the bad guy, but he'd gotten his teeth in again and they'd won. His main concern at the moment was wondering where his favorite rubber Kong ball was. He loved his partner, and was glad to see her, but she was forgetting the most important thing.

*   *   *

Erin wasn't sure what to expect at the Barley Corner. She was Carlyle's girl, and Mickey wasn't likely to have many friends there tonight, but she was still a cop. Mickey had been one of their own and she'd killed him. She didn't think anyone would attack her, but they might not exactly welcome her with open arms, either.

"Maybe you'd better let me go first," she said to her mom.

"It's not my first time in a bar, dear," Mary said. "You might be surprised to know some of the places I went with your father when we first started seeing one another."

"Mom! I don't need to know that!"

"Our first kiss, in the alley behind that bar in Brooklyn…" Mary went on dreamily.

"Mom!" Erin said again. Then she saw the twinkle in her mother's eye. "Okay, okay. But this place can be a little rough."

"You're forgetting I've been here before," Mary said. "I met that pleasant young man, Corky Corcoran."

"Don't remind me," Erin muttered. "And don't start about Corky. Just stick close and don't talk to any strange men."

Mary smiled. "You sound like me back when you were a teenager. Everything's all right, dear. Shelley's safe, you're fine, and your dog's going to be fine too. I know it may take some time to relax, but it's over."

"Nothing's over, Mom. Not yet."

"I do wish you'd leave your work at the station, dear. Your father was the same way after a difficult day." Mary clucked her tongue. "Your husband won't thank you for bringing it home with you."

"I don't have a husband."

"Yet."

Erin rolled her eyes and opened the Corner's front door. Better to walk right in like she owned the place than to skulk in the back way. Let them see her standing tall. They'd be more likely to respect that.

The pub was full almost to capacity, buzzing with conversation. The TVs were on, but no one was paying the slightest attention to the European soccer match. Some of the faces Erin saw looked tense and worried, but the general atmosphere was more relaxed than it had been.

"Hey! There she is!" someone shouted. Heads turned toward her. Men were smiling, waving to her. One guy stuck two fingers in his mouth and gave a loud, appreciative whistle.

Erin smiled uncertainly, thinking that she might be the only person in New York to get such a warm reception from police officers and gangsters in the same evening. What was going on? These might be mostly Carlyle's guys, but Mickey had been one of them and she'd killed him.

"Make a hole, fellas," somebody said. A pair of enormous guys, almost as big as Mickey, shouldered the crowd aside, making a gap for her. She recognized Robbie "Express" Exley and his buddy Wayne McClernand, truck drivers who worked for Corky. They weren't exactly harmless, but they were definitely allies.

"Wayne," she said. "And Express. How's it going?"

"Kickin' it old-school," Wayne said. "I heard you and Corks took care of business. Your dog okay? Looks like he's walkin' a little funny."

"Don't mind Rolf," she said. "He's just drunk."

Wayne guffawed. "And who's this you got with you?"

"This is my mom. Mom, this is Wayne and Robbie."

"Folks call me Express," Robbie said, touching two fingers respectfully to his forehead.

"Mary O'Reilly," Mary said. "Are you gentlemen friends of Mr. Carlyle's?"

"Yes ma'am," Wayne said. "We're in the delivery business. It was my privilege to give your daughter and a couple friends a lift to the city one time."

Erin was close enough now to see the bar through the crowd. Carlyle's traditional seat was empty. Despite the large number of patrons, nobody would dare take his stool. She turned to Wayne.

"Where's Carlyle?" she asked.

"In the back room," Wayne said. "He went in there with the old man about half an hour ago."

"Evan's here?" Erin asked sharply.

"What's the matter, dear?" Mary asked.

"I'll let you into the upstairs suite," Erin said. "Dad and the kids should still be there. I'll be up in a couple minutes. Don't come looking for me. I'm serious."

Mary wanted to ask questions, but Erin steered her to the door and got her through it. Wayne and Express trailed after her.

"We got a problem, ma'am?" Express asked. He flexed his massive arms slightly as he said it.

She was touched. In the Life, a guy who was willing to jump into a fight alongside you, no questions asked, was a valuable ally. "I don't think so," she said. "How'd Mr. O'Malley seem when he got here?"

"You know him," Express said with a shrug. "You can't read nothin' off him."

"Who was with him?"

"He had that chick with the big..." he began, cupping his hands in front of his chest. Then he remembered who he was talking to and stammered, turning slightly pink. "You know, the blonde. Vickie Blackburn. And Finnegan, you remember him? And a couple muscle guys. Plus Snake."

"Snake?" she repeated.

"Yeah. You know, Snake," Wayne said unhelpfully. "From Jersey. He just got in."

"I haven't met him," she said.

"Oh." Wayne looked suddenly uncomfortable. "Well, you'd remember him if you'd met him."

"What's he doing here?"

"Whatever the old man tells him."

"Right." Erin realized she wasn't going to get anything more out of these guys. "I better get back there." She walked to the back hallway. Outside the door to the room, she paused, made sure no one was looking, and squeezed her underwire through her shirt, turning on the hidden recorder. She wondered if she was about to make a recording of her last moments on Earth.

The back room at the Corner was used for two things: meetings and card games. Sometimes those were the same thing. It was a fairly small space, dominated by a green baize-topped card table surrounded by chairs. Carlyle sat in one of those chairs, opposite Evan O'Malley. Evan's face was completely unreadable. On Evan's right was a stranger, a slender, black-haired man with very dark eyes and a terribly scarred face. The whole right side of his head was puckered and pitted with what looked to Erin like the marks of long-healed third-degree burns. He was holding a black leather briefcase on his lap. Kyle Finnegan was on the other side of the stranger with his usual vacant, faraway look and uncombed hair. On Evan's left was Veronica Blackburn. The madam was as made-up as ever, but her eyes were bloodshot. She looked both frightened and angry. Behind the O'Malley chieftain stood a matched pair of goons, arms crossed. The atmosphere of the room was tense.

Carlyle stood up at once, followed a moment later by Evan and his damaged friend. "Good evening, darling," Carlyle said. "I'm glad you've joined us. I'd have called, but I thought you'd still be recuperating."

Evan extended a hand to Erin, his Notre Dame class ring glinting in the dim light. "It's a pleasure, Miss O'Reilly," he said. "I'm sorry for your troubles. I hope your sister-in-law is recovering well from her experience?"

"Thanks," Erin said, shaking his hand. "She's had a difficult time."

"So I understand," Evan said. "Is she in need of anything? Anything at all?"

"She's getting the best possible care," Erin said. "Thanks for asking."

"Some flowers, perhaps?"

"No, sir. Flowers would not be a good idea right now." She could only imagine how her brother would take that.

"If there's anything she requires, please let me know," he said. "And yourself?"

"I'm fine."

"This is Gordon Pritchard," Evan said, nodding to the scarred man at his side. "He'll be performing some of the services previously provided by the late Mr. Connor."

"Pleased to meet you, ma'am," Pritchard said. His voice was hoarse and raspy, suggesting he'd suffered an injury to his vocal cords, but under that was the same Belfast brogue she knew so well from Carlyle and Corky. Here was another Irish immigrant, she'd bet on it. The hand he offered Erin was sheathed in a black leather glove, though his other hand was bare. When she shook with him, she felt some odd ridges through the glove and wondered what that hand would look like.

"You know Mr. Finnegan and Ms. Blackburn, of course," Evan added.

"Ill met by moonlight, proud Titania," Finnegan said.

Erin blinked. "I'm sorry?"

"About, about, in reel and rout, the death-fires danced at night," Finnegan said. "The water, like a witch's oils, burnt green and blue and white. Or maybe an Irish poet instead? Summer surprised us."

"Are you feeling okay?" Erin asked. Finnegan had taken a tire iron to the head outside Detroit a few years ago and had been a little strange ever since.

"I will show you fear in a handful of dust." Finnegan shook his head and blinked. "Never better. Thanks for asking."

Veronica gave Erin an ambiguous look that contained a lot of complicated emotions. She didn't offer her hand, nor did Erin. The moment stretched out uncomfortably.

"Please, have a seat," Carlyle said, motioning to the place at his right. Erin sank down gratefully. Her headache hadn't gone away. If anything, it was getting worse. The loud talk in the Corner's main room hadn't helped. But it looked like she wasn't about to be murdered, at least. Rolf settled beside her.

The O'Malleys returned to their chairs. Erin tried not to stare at Pritchard. So this must be Evan's replacement muscle guy, the man Express called Snake. He was obviously dangerous, but where Mickey had been physically intimidating, Pritchard was colder, more calculating. Erin knew she'd have to keep an eye on him.

"So, you're up from Jersey?" she said to Pritchard.

"Just drove in," he said.

"I guess you'll be here going forward," she said.

"That's up to Mr. O'Malley," Pritchard said. "I go where I'm needed."

"We were just discussing the resolution of the late unpleasantness," Carlyle said.

"I apologize," Evan said, astonishing Erin. "Mr. Connor was under my employ, but I had no idea he would do what he did. Obviously, I'm appalled by his actions, and I'm grateful to you for taking care of the situation. I believe Mr. Pritchard has something you may find useful in aiding your recovery."

Pritchard laid the briefcase on the table, pivoted it so the handle was toward Erin, and slid it across the baize toward her.

She opened the case and saw it was packed with stacks of bills, twenties and hundreds, neatly bundled with elastic bands around them. She felt the bizarre urge to pick up one of the stacks and riffle through it, but resisted.

"What's this for?" she asked.

"Services rendered," Evan said. "You've become a valued associate, Miss O'Reilly, and I owe you thanks. I haven't forgotten what happened earlier, and I won't."

She knew he didn't know about the wire. If he had, she'd probably already be dead. But even so, Evan was being careful not to say anything specific, probably out of habitual paranoia.

"Forget about it," she said, trying to sound as much like a gangster as possible without overdoing it. "I did what I had to do."

"I couldn't agree more," Evan said. "There's been bad blood between Mr. Connor and the two of you."

"Corky, too," Erin added.

"Of course," Evan said. "I assume you're apprised of his status?"

"He just got winged," she said. "He'll be fine."

"The lad's luck would make a leprechaun blush," Carlyle said.

"This animosity has been getting in the way of business," Evan went on. "I've asked all of you here tonight to make sure this hatchet is buried. Mr. Pritchard will take over Mr. Connor's responsibilities, effective immediately. All other business will continue uninterrupted. No one is to take any retaliatory action, of any kind whatever, without my knowledge and approval. Is that quite clear?"

"Aye," Carlyle said. "As far as I'm concerned, the matter's concluded."

"I've got no beef with anyone here," Veronica said, shrugging. "Plenty of men come and go in my life. I've freed up some space in my calendar, that's all."

Erin looked hard at her and wondered. Had Veronica's fling with Mickey been purely a business arrangement? She had no idea. All she knew was that she'd be more careful around Veronica in the future.

"I'm glad to hear it," Evan said. "Now, does anyone have anything they'd like to add?"

"Did you see anything?" Finnegan asked Erin. "When you were between worlds? What did they say to you?"

"What did who say?" she asked.

"Them," he said. Then he leaned forward conspiratorially. "If they told you to do things, don't listen to them. They like to make mischief for its own sake. You can't trust them."

"I'll keep that in mind," she said.

"We won't take any more of your time," Evan said, standing up. He shook hands with Carlyle, then with Erin again. "Good evening. I expect further success in our joint ventures."

"Good night, sir," Erin said. She saw the relief in Veronica's face. The other woman hadn't known whether she was going to come out of this meeting alive either, she realized with a shock. And maybe, if Erin or Carlyle had said or done anything to cast suspicion on Veronica, Mickey's former squeeze would have died right there.

The more Erin saw of the Life, the more she figured out how precarious the whole thing was. Suspicion could equal guilt, and guilt was often paid off with a bullet. With that thought running through her head, Erin also felt a sense of relief when the door closed behind Evan and his entourage. She let out a breath she hadn't known she'd been holding.

"That's over," Carlyle said. "Let's go see to your kin."

"I think maybe I need a drink first," Erin said.

"That's a grand idea, darling."

Chapter 18

"That's better," Erin said. The whiskey nestled in her belly like a hot coal, radiating warmth through her insides. She set down the empty glass and glanced over at Carlyle, who was flipping through the contents of the briefcase. "How much is it?"

"A hundred, more or less," he said, closing the briefcase again. "That's a good year's salary for you, unless I'm mistaken."

"Including overtime," she said. "Evan's grateful, huh?"

"We did save his life," he reminded her.

"Along with our own. It wasn't completely selfless."

"That's not the point."

"What is the point? Guys in your world are always working an angle. Nobody just gives anything away."

"*Our* world," he gently corrected her. "Evan's thinking you're a sound investment."

"What a relief," she said sourly. "That's why I did all this, you know. So Evan O'Malley would like me."

He put a hand on hers. "I know why you did it, darling. And so do your kin. Who cares what the rest of them think? This only helps us. Now Evan knows you'll kill for cash."

She snatched her hand back. "I didn't do it for money! You know damn well I didn't!"

"But you took the money when he gave it to you," he said, unperturbed. "That's the same thing in his book."

"So he'll ask me to do it again. Then what do I do?"

"We cross the bridge that's in front of us, darling. No point borrowing tomorrow's troubles. Now, I'm thinking your mum and da will be wanting to see you. Shall we?"

Erin's phone buzzed. She fished it out and looked ruefully at the shattered screen. The name "Leo" stared back at her.

"Shit. I better take this," she said, thumbing the screen. "O'Reilly."

"Can you talk?" Phil Stachowski asked. He sounded anxious.

"I'm with Carlyle," she said.

"We need to meet," he said. "As soon as possible."

She'd been expecting this ever since her conversation with Keane and Holliday, but it still hit her like a fist to the gut. He was going to tell her how they were going to close down the undercover operation. He was going to sign Carlyle's death warrant, and maybe hers, too.

She sucked in a deep breath. "Nowhere too close to the Barley Corner," she said, marveling at the steadiness in her voice. "How about Liberty Park?"

"I can be there in half an hour," Phil said. "Anything you need?"

"Better make it an hour," she said. "I need to talk to my family."

"Of course. Be safe." He hung up.

"More goddamn meetings," she growled, stuffing her phone back in her pocket. "Okay, I'm still on the clock, I guess. Let's go up."

* * *

"Rolfie!" Anna exclaimed, rushing toward the dog.

The K-9 braced his front legs and lowered his head to take the impact. Erin winced, remembering the dog's injuries.

"Be gentle, kiddo," she said. "Rolf got hurt today."

Anna skidded to a stop. "Oh no!" she said, gingerly patting the Shepherd on the head. "Did he get shot?"

"No," Erin said. "An enormous criminal bounced him off the wall a couple times."

"Rough night, hey, kiddo?" Erin's dad said. He was sitting in Carlyle's armchair with a newspaper, a cup of coffee, and a double-barreled hunting shotgun on the table in front of him.

"You could say that," Erin said. "Geez, Dad, circle the wagons. Were you expecting an Indian attack?"

Sean O'Reilly got to his feet and she saw he was wearing his old service revolver on his hip. "I figured I better be prepared," he said. "Your mom's been filling me in on what happened. You think they'll send Shelley home tonight?"

Erin nodded. "She's just shaken and scared, not injured. Junior's with her right now. I'm sure they'll be here soon. Where's Mom?"

"In the kitchen," he said with a smile. "Making pies, of course."

"I'd best pay my respects," Carlyle said, leaving the room.

"Where does it hurt, Rolfie?" Anna asked, kneeling in front of the dog and beginning an amateur but thorough examination.

Rolf sat aloof, pretending he'd never heard of such a thing as pain.

"What about Patrick?" Erin asked.

"Asleep," Sean said. "I put him in the bedroom. There's only the one bed in the place."

"Dad," she hissed. "I'm thirty-six years old. If you think you still get to judge me based on where I sleep—"

He held up a hand. "I just meant, I could sleep on the couch, but we'll need to put Mary up somewhere, along with Junior and his family."

"They can go home," she said. "The crime scene's out in the street, not in the house."

"You think they'll be able to sleep there tonight?" He raised his eyebrows. "Would you?"

"Good point," she sighed. "And the front door needs to be replaced. I guess we'd better get them a hotel, or else see if Michael and Sarah can take some of you in." Erin's middle brother also lived in Manhattan, but he and his wife didn't have much extra space in their overpriced apartment. "And you don't need to stand guard here, Dad. This place is a fortress. Besides, I'm fine."

"Are you?" He looked her over. "You ought to still be in the hospital, kiddo. You know there's no shame in taking a breather. Looks like you and Rolf could both use it."

"The case isn't done," she said.

"I thought all these dirtbags were in lockup," he said. Then, glancing at Anna, he lowered his voice and added, "Or the morgue."

"It's complicated, Dad."

"Isn't it always? And you wonder why I stayed in Patrol. You gold shield types just tie yourselves in knots all day long." His tone was light, but his eyes were worried. "Seriously, kiddo. I hear you had another OIS."

He was deliberately using the acronym for Officer-Involved Shooting in the hopes Anna wouldn't pick up on it. The girl was engrossed in playing veterinarian with Rolf and took no notice.

"Yeah," Erin said.

"You feeling okay? This is, what, your third?"

"Depends," she said. "It's the second confirmed. There's a couple others I hit, but so did other people."

"That's a lot of weight to carry," he said. "Most officers never even put down one bad guy."

She shrugged. "I did what I had to do. I'm not second-guessing myself."

"Good. I know you wouldn't have done it if there'd been another way."

"Dad?"

"What is it, kiddo?"

"I wanted to." She swallowed. "I was thinking about it all the way there, hoping he'd give me a reason. What if... what if he'd given up? Would I have taken him in?"

"Of course you would," he said, putting his hands on her shoulders. She winced as his left hand caught her directly on her bruise. "We're judged by what we do, Erin. Not what we want to do. Thank God."

She nodded. "I guess it doesn't matter. He was never going to come quietly."

"What are you talking about?" Anna asked.

"Work, kiddo," Erin said.

"Oh." Anna made a face. "Is Mommy going to be here soon? I want to go home."

Erin looked at Sean. He looked back at her. She opened her mouth.

The door buzzer saved her from whatever comforting lie she'd been concocting. Erin started for the stairs. Her sense of balance momentarily deserted her and she lurched sideways, only barely catching herself.

"You stay here," Sean said firmly. "Sit down. I'll get the door." He headed downstairs, unsnapping the strap over his .38 on the way.

Erin thought about protesting but realized her dad was right. She really was tired. She sank down on the couch, wondering who could possibly be ringing Carlyle's doorbell, and what they'd think about an overprotective retired cop answering the door.

Her father gave a cry of surprise, which brought her right back to her feet before she had time to register the happiness in his voice. Then she heard her brother say something in reply, and a moment later, Sean Junior and Michelle came into the living room with her dad.

Both of them looked completely emotionally wrung out. Michelle's eyes were red and puffy. Her husband's jaw was set so firmly Erin could practically hear his teeth grinding from across the room. Michelle was wearing an oversized men's shirt—probably Vic's—and scrub pants too big for her.

None of that mattered a bit to Anna. "Mommy!" she shrieked. Rolf scrambled awkwardly out of the way in the nick of time. Then Michelle had her arms around her daughter, lifting her clean off the ground, clutching the girl tightly. Both of them started crying.

"Oh my God," Michelle murmured, covering Anna's face with kisses. "Oh God, oh God. My little angel."

Movement at the corner of Erin's eye made her look toward the kitchen. There was Mary, sleeves rolled up, dusted with flour, tears in her eyes, beaming. Behind her stood Carlyle, smiling wearily.

Erin's dad offered his hand to his son. "Glad to see you, Junior," he said gruffly, trying and failing to blink away his own tears. "How are you holding up?"

"I'll be okay," Sean Junior said. He darted a look Erin's direction that held shame and residual anger. He wasn't all right, she knew, but he was asking her to let it be for tonight.

She would, of course. The flaw in her brother's marriage wasn't her secret to spill.

A small, shy figure emerged from the bedroom. There was Patrick, still holding his constant companion through the chaos of the day, the fluffy plush sheep.

"Mom," he said quietly.

Michelle, without letting go of her daughter, went down on one knee and put out her other arm, bringing her son into her embrace.

Watching them, Erin rubbed at her own eyes to dry them and thought that maybe, just maybe, they'd all be okay. She went to the kitchen doorway.

"I have to go out for a bit," she said. "Work."

"You should be resting, dear," Mary said doubtfully.

"I promise, I'll go straight to bed as soon as this is over," she said. "I'll leave Rolf here. He's a little beat up."

"Are you armed?" Carlyle asked.

"No."

"Get something from one of the lads downstairs," he suggested. "Bobby at the front door ought to have a spare. He seems the sort."

She gave him a look. "You understand if I find an unregistered firearm on one of these guys, I'm legally obligated to arrest him."

He shrugged. "I'd feel better knowing you'd some protection about you, darling."

"Got you covered, kiddo," her dad said. He unbuckled his belt and slid the holster off it, extending his .38 to her.

"You sure about that, Dad?" she said.

"Of course," he said gruffly. "Got a spare in my overnight bag. Go on, take it."

"Thanks." She fastened it to her own belt next to her shield.

"What kind of meeting is this?" Mary asked, suddenly suspicious.

"I'm talking to another cop," she said.

"She ought to be fine," Mary said.

Carlyle nodded doubtfully. "As you will, darling. I'll see you after."

She held up the briefcase. "I'll take care of this while I'm out."

"What's in there, dear?" Mary asked.

"Papers," Erin said. "For work." That was technically true.

She slipped past the happy reunion and out of the apartment. The whiskey had dulled her headache, but she could still feel it waiting at the back of her skull. She really hoped this would be the last thing she'd need to do on this endless, exhausting day.

*   *   *

Phil was waiting for Erin at Liberty Park. He was dressed casually in jeans and a polo shirt under an open tweed coat. He was standing next to the memorial pool, staring into the depths. Lights behind the waterfalls were reflected off his eyeglasses.

Erin felt a little strange coming here. The memorial to the 9/11 attacks was still fairly new. When she looked at the pool, she saw a black hole in the heart of her city. Maybe that was the point. She felt hollowed out, empty.

"Evening," she said quietly, walking up to stand beside Phil.

"Evening," he said. "Your dog isn't with you. Is he okay?"

"Nothing that won't mend."

He turned to face her. "I heard some of what happened," he said. "I thought you were in the hospital."

"I checked myself out."

"I know. I called Bellevue this evening. Missed you by a few minutes."

"You shouldn't have done that," she said. "Nobody's supposed to know we're connected."

"I was worried. Don't worry, I wouldn't have come in person."

"That's sweet, Phil. Nice to know you care."

He let her sarcasm slide off him. "Erin, we're shutting it down."

"That's what Holliday told me," she said. "But it's a mistake."

"We've got no choice, Erin," he said softly. There was no anger in his face, only concern. "When an undercover gets compromised and their family ends up in the line of fire, we have to end the op. Otherwise it's only a matter of time before someone gets killed."

"People *did* get killed," she said. "One of ours plus three wiseguys. And it's only dumb luck we didn't lose more. We've got another cop in the hospital along with Ian Thompson. Both of them damn near died. Not to mention Corky and that poor cab driver. But we can't stop now."

"This was a direct attack on you," Phil said. "We can't let that go."

"I didn't let it go. Mickey's dead, damn it! I blew his brains out!"

"You're saying that like it's a good thing."

"That he's dead? Damn right it is! He was going to torture, rape, and murder my brother's wife, Phil! He tried to take out Evan O'Malley, too."

"What?" Phil apparently hadn't heard that part of the story.

"Mickey was supposed to meet with Evan, Carlyle, and me at noon." *Jesus*, she thought. Had that really been less than twelve hours ago? She'd had days that had felt long before, but this was one for the record books. "A bomb was planted under the table in the meeting room."

"I didn't hear about that."

"That's because Rolf found the bomb and Carlyle disarmed it. We didn't make the news."

"Where's the bomb now?"

Erin opened her mouth, realized she didn't have an answer for him, and closed it again. "I don't know. I guess Carlyle's still got it," she said weakly. "In all the excitement, I lost track of it. I'll give it to Skip Taylor first thing tomorrow."

"So you're saying there were two attempts on your life," Phil said. "*Today*. This isn't exactly strengthening your argument."

"Evan put out a contract on Mickey. A hundred grand. He paid me this evening. In cash."

"You got *a hundred thousand dollars* from Evan O'Malley?"

She handed over the briefcase. "I didn't get an exact count yet, but every cent I got is in there. I'm in, Phil. Evan thinks I'm all the way in. He thinks I'll kill for him. We can use this."

He shook his head. "I'm not going to stand here and let you put your family in more danger, Erin."

"Can you guarantee me, with what we've got right now, that we'll get all the O'Malleys?" she shot back. "All their middle and upper bosses? Every last one? Because if we don't, if one of them slips through, that's the ball game. Carlyle's dead unless he disappears, and now so am I. I'm a gangster now, Phil. I took money for a hit. I'm in the Life as far as they're concerned. The only way I get out is if we make a clean sweep. So are we ready?"

Phil's jaw tightened. "Not yet," he said. "And you know it. We still need O'Malley's accounts. That's the only way we'll know for sure we've got all the loose ends tied up. Choke off the money and the organization dies. Carlyle has told me he doesn't know all of Evan's business dealings and connections. And new guys keep showing up in the picture. This is a very large, sprawling case."

"I know," she said. "I met a new guy less than two hours ago. Gordon Pritchard, out of Jersey. You heard of him?"

"The name's familiar," he said. "I think Carlyle's mentioned him, but I'd have to check the case notes. Who is he?"

"Mickey's replacement. Not as big. Skinny, black hair, nasty scars on his face. Goes by Snake."

"I'll look into him."

"So will I. But here's the thing, Phil. I can't be looking out for guys like him the rest of my life. If I run now, I'll never know if I'm safe or not, and I will not live that way. And I'm sure as shit not going to throw my life away in WitSec. You copy?"

"I copy," he sighed. "So what am I supposed to tell your Captain?"

"Tell him the op's still on. Tell him I'm in with the O'Malleys. You keep saying you've got my back, Phil. Here's your chance to prove it. Fight for me. I can bring this home. I swear."

"And what about your family?"

"I'm doing this for them," she said grimly. "If you let Holliday shut us down now, they lose me, either dead or in Witness Protection for the rest of my goddamn life."

He looked at her for an endless minute, searching her face. She heard the faint flow of water from the memorial.

Then, finally, he nodded once. "Okay, Erin. I'll stick my neck out for you. I hope neither one of us is making a mistake. But I trust your judgment." A faint smile creased his face. "Even if you did check yourself out of the hospital against your doctor's advice."

She smiled too, feeling blessed relief wash through her. "All I got was a good crack on the head. Give me a night's rest and I'll be fine."

"Do you want to talk about it? About what happened at the Domino Refinery?"

Erin shook her head. "Not now. I'll spill it to Doc Evans next time I meet with him. I don't need you to be my shrink, Phil. Just have my back."

"I've always got your back." He shifted the briefcase to his left hand and offered his right. "You're a good cop, Erin, and you've got guts to spare. Just remember, you don't have to do all this by yourself."

"Who says I'm alone?" she said. "I've still got Rolf, don't I?"

Chapter 19

When Erin woke up early the next morning, she had pain in parts of her body she hadn't even known existed. All the bumps, scrapes, and bruises she'd gotten in her fight with Mickey, little things she hadn't noticed at the time, were clamoring for her attention. Her headache was a little better, but her arm hurt worse than before. She could hardly use it. Her cheek felt swollen and puffy. She had an enormous bruise on her hip, another on her elbow, and a sore neck where he'd grabbed her. If she let herself, she could still feel the pressure of his gigantic hand around her throat.

She gingerly eased out of bed and went into the kitchen. The apartment felt empty. The rest of the O'Reillys had departed last night for a hotel. Rolf padded behind her and stood in the doorway, head cocked, seeing what she would do. He also looked a little stiff. Erin opened the freezer and got out the ice tray. She popped half a dozen cubes out of the tray, put them in a plastic bag, and held the icepack against her arm. She tossed another cube onto the floor, where Rolf proceeded to lick it back and forth across the linoleum.

"Awake, darling?" Carlyle asked. He'd quietly wrapped himself in his silk bathrobe and followed her to the kitchen.

"Look who's talking," she said. "I hurt too much to sleep. And when I wake up, I start thinking."

He nodded. "I've been worrying about Ian," he said. "Poor lad. Do you suppose they'd let me in to see him?"

"Not yet," she said. "He'll be under guard until the DA's office decides what to do with him."

"Surely they'll not charge him," Carlyle said.

"He killed two people."

"Criminals who were engaged in a serious crime."

"I know that. Look, if it was up to me, he'd get a damn medal, okay? I'll talk to Webb and see what we can do for him. Then I'll get to the hospital to check on him. He should be awake."

"I'll thank you for it, darling." Carlyle's face was drawn and tired. "I tell you, Erin, to lose Siobhan the way I did, and then to see Ian there in the street... I thought I'd lost him, too, and it near broke me."

She went to him and held him, disregarding her aching body's protestations. "He's tough," she said. "I've never seen a man who's harder to kill. He'll pull through."

"I shouldn't have asked it of him," he said.

"You didn't. He volunteered. You told him not to get in a gunfight. This was Ian's choice and I don't care what the DA says, he did the right thing. I just wish he'd put one in Mickey's face while he was at it. You were right about Mickey. He needed to be killed, and if it'd happened sooner, it would've saved us all a lot of trouble and pain."

"Nay, Erin, you were right," Carlyle said. "If you'd let me take care of him, it would have brought the both of us down. You've got me walking the right path now. Don't go second-guessing yourself or I just may fall off it and drag you down with me."

"But what about the cops who got shot? And Shelley? They'd have all been fine. People are *dead* because of him!"

"Not at the cost of your soul, darling," he said. "Don't put all that on yourself. Mickey made his choices, and if there's any justice at all, he'll spend the rest of eternity paying for them. But that's not up to us. You can't kill a lad because of what you're afraid he might do, and you can't make choices in hindsight."

"I guess not. But I wish I could." She sighed and ran her good hand through her hair. "Thanks for watching the kids yesterday. It was a big help."

"I should've been with you, darling. I could have done more, I'm thinking."

"Besides saving our lives with that bomb? And finding out where Mickey was hiding? You did plenty. We couldn't have done it without you." She leaned in and kissed him lightly. "Now I'd better get to work. I need to talk to Vic and Webb as soon as I can. And I'll need the bomb."

For a second, he looked blank. Then he laughed.

"Aye, that. I'd clean forgot. It's in the cellar. I'll fetch it out for you. While you're away, what shall I do if the O'Reilly clan comes calling?"

"You deal with gangsters all the time. You telling me you can't handle my mom and dad? Use your imagination."

He smiled. "Fair point, darling. I'll keep the home fires burning."

"Oh, one other thing. Can I get something from the bar on my way? A nice bottle?"

"Don't you think it's a mite early for that sort of thing, darling?"

"It's not for me. It's for a friend."

*   *   *

The sun was just barely over the horizon and the Manhattan streets were still dark, the shadows of skyscrapers blotting out the light, when Erin and Rolf got to the Eightball. It was a measure of Erin's pain and fatigue that in spite of her increased paranoia she took the elevator up from the parking garage instead of the stairs. She wondered if this was how it felt to get old, to have every joint and muscle aching all the time. That didn't bode well for her future. She told herself she'd have taken the stairs if she hadn't had things to carry. She was holding a cardboard box with a bomb and a bottle in it.

She stepped out of the elevator into the Major Crimes office thinking of stimulants. She'd have to fire it up, but the coffee machine was there in the break room: solid, faithful, waiting.

She stopped short. Someone else was also in the office, studying the whiteboard.

"Skip?" she said in surprise.

Skip Taylor turned with a grin. "Morning, Erin. Great to see you! I heard you were up and around. What's the damage?"

"Concussion and some bruises."

"That's not so bad," he said. "Hell, working EOD in the Sandbox, I think everybody in my squad had at least one concussion. Those damn IEDs going off all the time, we'd get bounced all over the place. If we hadn't had helmets, all our brains would've been oatmeal. But I wasn't expecting to run into you. Aren't you on admin leave? Or medical? Or both?"

"I assume so," she said. "I talked to IAB yesterday evening, and they said I was in the clear, but it'll probably be a day or two before they give me street duty and I get my guns back. What're you doing up here?"

"I came up to drop off my final report on the bomb in Connor's car," he said. "Figured I'd hang around and talk to

Lieutenant Webb when he showed up, see if you all need anything else from me."

"Actually, there is one thing," she said. She hefted the box Carlyle had given her on the way out the door.

"Ooh, genuine Irish whiskey," he said, reading the label.

"Don't get your hopes up," she said. "I live over a bar. This was the box we had handy. I want you to take a look at what's inside."

"What is it?" He bent over to take a peek.

"A bomb. And a bottle of liquor."

"Ha ha."

"I'm serious. Did you hear about the fire alarm at First Republic Bank yesterday?"

"There was a bomb at the bank?" Now Skip looked surprised. "Nobody called us."

"It didn't go off and it wasn't reported."

"Why not? If a cop finds a bomb, they're not supposed to handle it. I don't care if you've had demo training, Erin, you should've gotten the hell away and let me and my guys deal with it!"

"There wasn't time. Carlyle and I figured it was set to go off at noon and we only had a couple minutes. I didn't touch it until he'd disarmed it."

Skip held up his hand. "Wait a minute. You were at a bank with Cars Carlyle, the two of you found a bomb, and he just took it apart, tucked it under his arm, and walked out?"

"Pretty much. Rolf's the one who found it. It's a complicated situation, Skip. Can you just take a look at it? I guarantee you, it's safe."

"Famous last words," he snorted. "There's no such thing as a guaranteed safe bomb, any more than a guaranteed unloaded gun. Let's take it downstairs."

"You don't believe me?"

"I'm a veteran bomb technician who can still count to ten on my hands," Skip said. "All the trust in the world won't grow my fingers back. If I'm going to mess with some jackass's homemade science project, I'm going to do it the right way, in my lab, with my tools."

"Can I come?"

"Your funeral."

So Erin followed Skip down to the Bomb Squad's lab, still without her coffee. She left Rolf upstairs. The K-9 wanted to come with her, but she told him to stay. He grudgingly settled his battered body beside her desk for a morning snooze.

Skip laid the box on his wooden work table. He set out a large array of pliers, wire cutters, metal shears, and other tools Erin couldn't identify. He moved his table lamp over the box and turned it on. Then he just stared at the device for several silent minutes.

Finally, he deployed a box cutter and slit the box open at two corners, folding down the cardboard so he could see the bomb without lifting it out. Watching him, Erin remembered how she'd just plopped the thing in her car's passenger seat with hardly a second thought. She shivered.

"Okay," Skip said. He picked up the bomb and turned it over in his hands, studying it. "Simple device, no anti-tampering. This was amateur hour."

"So it's safe?"

"Of course it's not safe. It's a bomb that was made by some asshole who didn't have the slightest idea what he was doing. That makes it about the least safe thing on Earth. Why do you keep asking about safety, Erin? The *world* isn't safe! But our friend Cars did a good job. It should be okay. Looks like a standard gunpowder pipe bomb. Anything around it?"

"A bunch of ball bearings."

"Ouch. That'd make it an antipersonnel device with a lethal radius of, I'd say, about ten meters. But you wouldn't want to be within fifty if you could help it."

"How does it compare with the bomb in Mickey's car?" she asked.

Skip shook his head. "Totally different device. Different explosive, different detonator, different style. There's no way they were made by the same guy. Did you think they were from the same bomber?"

"No," she said. "But I had to check. I think Mickey Connor made this one."

"Retaliation?" he guessed.

"Yeah. He tried to kill Carlyle, Evan O'Malley, and me."

"Carlyle didn't make the bomb that took out Connor's car," Skip said. "I'm sure of it. But the guy who did it isn't as dumb as I thought."

"That's in your report?"

"Affirmative."

"Thanks, Skip. If you can write up what you've got on this bomb and send it to me, I'd appreciate it."

"Can do. Take it easy, Erin."

"Copy that." She started for the door, then remembered something and came back. She snatched up the bottle that had shared the box with Mickey's bomb. "This is coming with me."

"Damn." He grinned. "I was hoping you'd forget."

*　　*　　*

She was back upstairs in the office, going over Skip's report and savoring her second cup of coffee, when Webb and Vic arrived at almost the same time.

"What are you doing here?" Webb demanded.

"I work here," she said. "What's your excuse, sir?"

"You're supposed to be in the hospital."

"I'm going back there as soon as we've touched base."

"Is that a promise?"

"Yes, sir." She didn't intend to stay there, but she'd promised Carlyle she'd look in on Ian, so she was going back to the hospital. Technically.

He sighed and pointed to her coffee cup. "All right. Tell me there's more where that came from."

"The machine's warmed up."

While Webb poured his morning stimulant, Vic came over and sat on the edge of Erin's desk, his customary gigantic cup of Mountain Dew in hand.

"You know, I thought that big son of a bitch had killed you at first," he said conversationally.

"All he did was punch me in the head."

"Yeah, and I saw the size of his fists." He shook his head. "You think he was, like, a Cold War lab experiment who got loose? Maybe some crazy scientist grew him in a vat somewhere?"

"Have you been watching bad late-night sci-fi movies?"

"Maybe."

"I've got something for you."

"Uh oh. What sort of thing?"

She took out the bottle she'd gotten from the Barley Corner and handed it to him. He held it up and studied the label.

"Grey Goose Ducasse," he read aloud. "Erin, this is a hundred-dollar bottle of vodka. What the hell is this for?"

"You had my back," she said. "Every step of the way."

"That's my job," he said. "I already get paid. I can't accept this."

She shook her head. "You literally gave Michelle the shirt off your back. You didn't just help save her. You did it the right way. You've earned this. Besides, I know a bar owner. I got a discount."

"You know it's a felony bribing a cop, right?"

"It's only bribery if I want something in return."

"Okay, I'll drink it," he said. "Because it's the smoothest vodka there is, and passing it up would be a damn crime. But this doesn't mean I like your boyfriend."

"Of course not."

"And it doesn't mean I like you. You're still a crazy bitch."

"And you're still a meathead thug." She smiled at him.

"You two ought to resign, hand in your shields, and go into business together," Webb said. "You could write greeting card slogans. Now, who's going to tell me exactly what happened yesterday?"

"The bomb placed in Mickey Connor's car wasn't intended to kill him," Erin said. "It was planted to make him think Carlyle was trying to take him out. Mickey and Carlyle were already enemies. Mickey decided to retaliate. But he knew Evan O'Malley wouldn't approve a hit on Carlyle, not without better proof than Mickey had. So Mickey thought it was as good a time as any to take the old man out of the picture. He whipped up a remote-controlled pipe bomb. Then he agreed to a meeting with O'Malley, Carlyle, and me. Either he or one of his guys got there early and planted the bomb in the conference room we were set to use. Then he went after my family."

"Why hit your family?" Webb asked. "What's the point, if you were supposed to get blown up anyway?"

"I think Mickey had a couple of reasons," she said. "Shelley was his insurance policy, just in case the hit failed. Mickey was a murderous psycho, but he wasn't stupid. What if I didn't show to the meeting at all? What if I got delayed and wasn't in the room when the bomb blew? What if I got hurt, but not killed? It wasn't a sure thing. Shelley told me Mickey interrogated her about my family, my schedule, and my behavior patterns."

"He was planning to hit you," Webb said. "While keeping you at arm's length by holding your sister-in-law hostage."

"Not just her," she said grimly. "He was trying for my niece and nephew. If Ian hadn't been there, he would've gotten them, too."

"What an asshole," Vic said. "Connor, not Thompson. Thompson's kind of an asshole, too, but I don't think he'd kidnap a couple of kids."

Erin shot him a dirty look. "You promised not to trash-talk Ian until this case was over."

"I only said he was kind of an asshole," Vic said. "That description matches half the people in New York."

She let it go and turned to Webb. "What's going to happen to Ian?" she asked.

"Well, he did shoot two men in broad daylight," Webb said. "We've got him on dashcam doing it. Open and shut. But here's the thing. Those two men were engaged in a violent kidnapping. One of their associates gunned down our officers seconds later. And Thompson's legally registered to carry the gun he had on him. It appears he was being a Good Samaritan, trying to prevent a felony from being committed. He was badly wounded by NYPD officers. Though they were acting in good faith, the DA seems to think there's a potential liability issue."

"He's scared Thompson's gonna sue the city," Vic said with a cynical smile. "So he's not gonna bring charges, in return for Thompson being a good boy and staying away from the lawyers?"

"That's pretty much the shape of it," Webb said. "The optics of charging him would be really bad in any case. The District Attorney is a political animal, remember."

"Oh, I don't forget," Vic said. "And neither does he."

"So Ian walks?" Erin insisted.

"Assuming his leg mends properly," Webb said dryly. "Otherwise he limps. So, Connor hit your family's house and grabbed your sister-in-law. How did the two of you track him down?"

"Mickey caught a bullet in the firefight," she said. "I used my contacts to find a guy who treats criminals for gunshot wounds. Vic and I leaned on him. We learned Mickey had an unusual smell. I deduced from the smell that he'd been hiding out at a candy or sugar factory, probably an old, out-of-use facility."

"He was lying low so O'Malley wouldn't kill his treacherous ass," Vic added.

"I went back to my contacts and got a hot lead on the Domino Sugar Refinery," she continued. "We arrived to find James Corcoran already on scene. There was probable cause to enter, since I had reason to believe the two of them were likely to try to kill one another."

"What's Corcoran got to do with any of this?" Webb asked.

That was a question Erin didn't want to answer. "I'd rather this not go in the final report," she said slowly.

"Oh, Lord," Webb said, rubbing his temples.

"Corky was engaged in a flirtation with our kidnapping victim," she said. "It hadn't been, um, consummated, but he had an emotional investment in the situation."

"So your sister-in-law was getting it on with a gangster, too," Vic said.

"Not exactly," she said. "But that was what it looked like. That's how Mickey became aware of my connection to Shelley. He was following her from a liaison with Corky and saw me meet with her."

"So to Connor's mind, she was involved in the Life," Webb said. "And a legitimate target."

"Yes, sir. Anyway, I've given my report on the shooting to Lieutenant Keane and Captain Holliday, but to keep it short, Mickey jumped me, I shot him, he punched me, and I shot him again."

"He was wearing a vest," Vic said. "I've got Levine's preliminary report here. She says the two you put in his chest didn't penetrate the Kevlar. She also says he was coked out of his mind, so he probably didn't even feel them hit him."

"He got the cocaine from the doc who treated him," Erin said. "No wonder he just kept coming."

"That head shot was the only thing that would've put him down fast," Vic agreed. "A guy that big, wearing body armor and drugged up, would've gone down like Tony Montana in *Scarface*. You know that scene? 'Say hello to my little friend?'"

"Everybody knows that scene," Erin said. "People who've never seen the movie know that scene. Your Pacino impression needs work."

"So I just have one question," Webb said.

The two other detectives looked inquiringly at him.

"Who put the bomb in Connor's car?" he asked. "Who set this whole thing off?"

"I don't know for sure," Erin said. "But I think Vinnie the Oil Man had it done. He didn't do it himself, but he's the guy who'd benefit most from an internal struggle in the O'Malleys. I think he used someone on the inside."

"Who?" Vic asked.

She shrugged. "No idea."

"That's an interesting theory, O'Reilly," Webb said. "But it's a little—"

"Thin," all three of them chorused.

"All I know," she said, "is somebody fired Mickey Connor straight at Carlyle and me like a goddamn guided missile. It has to be someone with enough understanding of the O'Malleys' inner workings to know what buttons to press. This wasn't a simple gangland hit. This was planned by somebody who's smart, capable, and dangerous."

"Sounds like you think they'll try again," Webb commented.

She nodded. "Yeah."

"But we have no evidence pointing to a particular suspect."

"No, sir."

"Well, no one died in the bombing," Webb said. "And the guy whose car got blown up is in the morgue right now. There won't be a lot of pressure to close this one. But I won't pretend I'm happy that some devious bastard took a run at one of my detectives. He didn't even have the guts to come straight at you. You're going to be jumping at shadows."

"I already was, sir. Comes with the Job."

"Don't worry, sir," Vic said. "The only reason her family got roped in was because Connor thought it was a good idea. With him out of the picture, they should be safe enough. And if anyone goes for her again, they'll have to get through the rest of us. I'm talking the whole NYPD. You got thirty-five thousand bodyguards, Erin. Plus your bad-ass mutt."

"And you," she added, smiling at him. "Now, if that's all, sir, I think I'd better get to the hospital."

"That's an excellent idea," Webb said. "I don't want to see you back in this office until you're officially cleared for duty. That's an order." He cracked a slight smile. "Get better. That's an order, too."

She returned the smile. "Copy that, sir."

Chapter 20

Ian Thompson lay in his hospital bed, eyes closed. He was very pale, but his color was a little better than yesterday. They'd pulled his tubes, another good sign.

Erin walked in as quietly as she could, going to his bedside. He didn't move, but she could feel the nervous tension radiating off his body. It was impossible to sneak up on the man, even as weak and wounded as he was.

"How are you feeling?" she asked quietly.

"I'll live." His voice was hoarse, an aftereffect of the tube they'd had down his throat.

"Are you hurting much?"

He opened his eyes. They were dull with pain, but she could see the alertness hidden deep inside. "Got morphine if I want it." He cocked his head slightly at a button which connected to a cable. The cable snaked its way to a machine linked to an IV drip.

"Using it?"

He shook his head.

"Why not?"

"Like to keep my head clear. Don't like drugs. Not important. What about the kids?"

"Kids?"

"Anna and Patrick. They okay?"

"The kids are fine. So is Shelley. Thanks to you."

Ian closed his eyes, hiding the relief in them. "That's good," he whispered.

"I've got more good news," Erin said, trying to be deliberately cheerful. "It looks like you're not going to be charged with anything. Lieutenant Webb talked to the DA and he says nobody wants to prosecute you. So you're not in any trouble. You can just concentrate on getting well."

He nodded again, but he didn't open his eyes. He didn't seem particularly thrilled by the news.

"Hey," she said, gently touching his right arm, the one that wasn't bandaged. "You did a good thing yesterday, Ian. You hear me? My brother's family is alive because of you."

He opened his eyes then and looked straight at her. "I didn't stop him," he said. "Connor got away from me with Mrs. O'Reilly. I should've had him."

"Bullshit," Erin said. "You got shot. Five goddamn times! You damn near died. But you stayed in the fight as long as anyone could. You took out two of Mickey's thugs. Those were guys Vic and I didn't have to deal with. You knocked out his getaway car, so he had to waste time getting another ride. And you winged him. If you hadn't, we wouldn't have been able to track him. The only lead I had was one I got from the doctor who stitched him up. Shelley would be dead if it wasn't for you, and Anna and Patrick along with her."

He nodded, but his eyes slid away from hers.

"Listen to me!" she snapped. "You saved my family! I'm trying to thank you."

"No thanks needed, ma'am."

"No," she said. "You don't get to call me that ever again. You took bullets for us, Ian. You're family, now and forever. So knock off the bullshit. You copy?"

"I copy... Erin."

"And if I know Shelley, as soon as you're up and around, she's going to insist you come over for dinner. She'll cook you the best damn meal you've ever eaten. You don't have to feel like you've earned it, but you're going to eat it and like it. And my mom's going to bake you pie. Lots and lots of pie."

"You're giving me a lot of orders," he said, but there was a hint of dark amusement hiding at the back of his eyes. "On what authority?"

"I told you. You're family. So that makes me your big sister, and you better not forget it."

He nodded. "Understood."

"Now I'm going to give you one more order. The same one my Lieutenant just gave me. Get well. Because I need you."

"This isn't over, is it," he said. It wasn't a question. "Connor's out of the picture, but you're not done yet."

"No," she said. "The guy who started this is still out there. This war isn't over. But we're going to win it, and when we do, I want you with me."

"Roger that, ma—Erin," he said, catching himself just in time. "You need me, I'm there."

"But for now, you better get some rest." She squeezed his hand. "Semper fi, Marine."

"Semper fi," he said.

Erin felt a little better as she left Ian's room. One known enemy was dead, an unknown one was no doubt making new plans, but she made a promise to herself. The next time anyone came for her or her family, Erin O'Reilly would be ready for them.

Keep reading for a sneak peek from
Bossa Nova

Here's a sneak peek from Book 16: Bossa Nova

Coming 6/27/22

"I'll have the fettuccine Alfredo," Cassie said. She nodded to Ben. "And he'd like the spaghetti with meatballs, child portion."

"And for you, ma'am?" the waitress asked Erin.

Erin had no idea what she wanted. "I'll get the same as him," she said.

"Children's size?" the waitress asked.

"No. Normal size."

As the rest of them ordered, Erin tried to bring her mind back to what she was supposed to be thinking about. This was the closest thing Ian could get to bringing his girl to meet the parents. They should be concentrating on Cassie, getting to know her. The nurse seemed like a nice enough woman. She was obviously pleasant, intelligent, and easy on the eyes. And Ian, despite his continued hypervigilance, was calmer around her. He even seemed happy. Erin glanced at him with a smile.

The smile fell off her face. Ian was paying no attention whatsoever to the waitress, or to his girlfriend. He was focused on something across the room. His eyes narrowed. Suddenly, with no warning whatsoever, he jumped to his feet. His chair tumbled backward. His coat was already open. His right hand dove inside. By the time it came out again, gripping his nine-millimeter Beretta, he was stepping around the back of Cassie's chair, shielding her with his body.

"Get down!" he shouted.

Erin had started moving in reaction to Ian, her police instincts kicking in, but she'd been a little sluggish. Before she could do anything, he was already up. She'd learned to trust Ian's awareness. She wasted no time asking for an explanation. Instead, she ducked, pulled up her right pants leg, and whipped out the snub-nosed .38 she always carried, on duty or off.

Someone screamed. Across the room, Erin saw a waiter running toward the kitchen and a man springing after him. In the man's hand was the sort of shape that every cop learned to recognize.

"Gun!" Erin shouted. Then she followed up with, "NYPD! Drop it!"

The gunman fired. Blood blossomed on the upper back of the waiter's white jacket, but the man kept running, flinging himself through the swinging doors and out of sight. Erin drew a bead on the shooter. However, the other restaurant patrons had now had time to realize they were witnessing a shooting and were panicking. Several civilians rushed across her line of fire.

She caught a quick glimpse of the shooter as he pursued the fleeing waiter. It was hard to tell what was going on. The dining room had turned into instant bedlam. Maybe twenty percent of the customers were being sensible and either hitting the floor or sitting very still. Everyone else was running, shouting, or both. She saw several cell phones being held next to diners' heads, so at least she could safely assume backup would be on the way as soon as Dispatch got the calls.

"Stay with them," Erin told Ian as she started for the kitchen.

He nodded, holding his pistol in a two-handed Weaver stance. "Go," he said, not bothering to look at her or the rest of their party. His attention was solely on the chaos across the room.

Cassie, Erin noted approvingly out of the corner of her eye, had gathered Ben into her arms and dropped under the table. Carlyle was crouched beside them. They ought to be okay. This had the looks of a personal attack, not a terrorist incident.

As Erin ran against the flow of terrified New Yorkers, she saw a man slumped over a table. Blood was pouring out of him. Another man, beside him, had grabbed a white cloth napkin and was holding it against the wounded man's neck. The napkin was already turning bright red.

She hesitated an instant, torn between two duties. But as long as there was an active shooter, her priority was to neutralize him. Other cops would be on site momentarily and could help administer first aid. She rushed into the kitchen, hearing two more gunshots as she ran.

Erin shouldered through the double-hinged doors and saw half a dozen cooks and wait staff, all looking stunned and frightened. She also saw a blood trail on the black-and-white checkerboard floor tiles. The irregular pattern of red spatter led straight through the kitchen and out the back door. She saw no sign of the gunman. Assuming he was chasing the man he'd shot, she followed the blood.

With a pang, she wished she hadn't left Rolf at home. Her K-9 partner was at his best in pursuit situations. He could have already caught up with the shooter and tackled him. But Rolf was lounging around the bedroom with one of his chew-toys, so Erin had to rely on her own two feet.

The door led her into a service hallway at the back of the restaurant. A bloody smear on the back door drew her to it. She went out in a rush, revolver at the ready, and saw an empty alley. The blood trail ended so abruptly that she knew the guy had to have gotten into a car, which had driven off.

Why would a waiter have a car waiting for him? And what had happened to the gunman? Erin stood frozen for a moment, perplexed. Something was going on that she didn't yet understand. But she could hear sirens and knew more cops were on their way. It was pointless to run down the alley and out into the street on the off-chance of snagging the shooter. Better to go back in and see what she could do for the victim who was still in the dining room.

She stepped back into the service corridor and nearly ran into a man in a black suit who had just emerged from another door. With a flash of recognition, she saw it was the guy who'd been chasing the waiter.

"Hands!" she shouted, throwing her gun in line and taking aim at his center of mass.

"Whoa, lady," the man said, showing two empty hands. "I don't know what you think is going on..."

"NYPD Major Crimes, asshole," she snapped. "Face the wall. Now!"

"I didn't do nothing," he protested, but he obeyed.

"Bullshit. I watched you shoot a guy less than two minutes ago!"

"Oh. Sounds like I'm in some trouble," he said, sounding less than concerned. "So you've got this guy you say I shot, and the gun you say I shot him with?"

Erin was reaching for her handcuffs when she remembered she was wearing her Sunday church clothes which did not, in fact, include a set of bracelets. She cursed silently and frisked the man anyway. She didn't find a gun on him, but she did find an empty holster on his belt.

"Care to explain this?" she demanded.

"Fashion accessory," he said. "All the cool kids are carrying them."

"Where's the gun?"

"What gun?"

"The gun you were carrying."

"I don't know what you're talking about."

"I'm talking about the holster you're wearing, for the gun I saw you use to shoot a man in the back! I'm talking about the gunpowder residue you've got on your hands and clothes."

"That's all circumstantial," he said glibly.

"What's your name? Or is that circumstantial, too?"

"Frank Vanzano, ma'am."

"Well, Frank Vanzano, you're under arrest for attempted murder, reckless endangerment, and illegal possession and discharge of a firearm. I've got a suspicion you know your rights, and this isn't the first time you've gone through this, but I'm going to read them to you anyway."

"You do what you gotta do, lady," Vanzano said. He'd been amped up when she'd first run into him, but now he just seemed bored.

The kitchen door flew open and a pair of uniformed officers burst through. Erin held up her hands, but made sure to step back from Vanzano and keep an eye on him.

"O'Reilly, Major Crimes!" she shouted, letting her revolver dangle from one finger by the trigger guard. The last thing she wanted was to get popped by an overeager rookie. She saw Vanzano tense for a moment, but the gunman decided against making a run for it.

"Where's your shield, ma'am?" one of the officers demanded.

"Pocket," she said. "I'm taking it out now."

She eased her gold detective's shield out slowly and showed it to them.

"And who's this mope?" the other cop asked, indicating Vanzano.

"He's the one who started shooting," she said. "We've got one casualty in the dining room and one who ran out the back."

"The guy in the dining room wasn't shot," the uniform said.

"He wasn't?" Erin hadn't expected that.

"No, ma'am. Somebody slit his throat. The knife was right there on the table next to him."

"Is he dead?"

"Don't know."

"Shit," Vanzano said.

"You know the guy?" Erin asked.

"I got nothing to say to you, lady. I want my phone call and my lawyer."

"Can you guys take custody?" she asked the uniforms.

"Copy that, Detective," the first cop said, pulling out his cuffs. Vanzano rolled his eyes and gave the ceiling a long-suffering look as the steel bracelets clicked shut around his wrists.

"Take him to the Eightball," she said. Then she slipped her .38 back into her ankle holster and headed back to the dining room.

The restaurant was louder and only slightly less panicked than it'd been when she'd left. Several uniformed officers were trying to restore order, but the patrons weren't making it easy for them. No paramedics had arrived yet, and Erin saw a couple of cops at the table with the wounded man. The guy who'd been holding the napkin against the other man's throat was now standing to one side with yet another cop talking to him. She noted he was also in handcuffs.

Carlyle, Ian, Cassie, and Ben were still at their table. They were standing now. Cassie was holding Ben in her arms. Ian no longer had his gun out, which was a good thing, considering how many law-enforcement officers were present. His left hand was resting on Cassie's shoulder in what was probably meant to be a comforting gesture, but his body language was fully activated and alert and his right hand remained empty and ready.

Erin clipped her shield to her belt so it was obvious. She crossed the room to rejoin her dinner companions.

"It's over now," she said to Cassie. "Nobody else is going to get hurt."

"What happened?" Cassie's voice was sharp with agitation and fear.

"Mob hit," Ian said. In contrast to her tone, he sounded perfectly calm.

Cassie looked from Ian to Erin. "Is he serious?"

"Usually," Erin said. "I think he's got a sense of humor, but it's pretty well camouflaged."

"But was it? A mob hit?"

"I don't know yet. And I need to get to work now, sorry. I have to duck out on dinner."

"Mommy," Ben said.

"What is it, honey?" Cassie asked.

"You're squeezing me."

"Sorry." Cassie loosened her grip a little, but Erin had the feeling she'd have to break the other woman's fingers to get her to let go of her son just then.

Carlyle stepped forward. "Erin must be about her duties," he said. "Why don't the rest of us go back to the Corner? I've rather lost my taste for Italian cuisine."

"I'll see you later," Erin said. "Nice to meet you, Cassie. Ben. I wish it was under better circumstances. But this is my job."

"I'm familiar with the aftereffects of violence," Cassie said. "I'm just not accustomed to watching it happen. I'd like to get my boy out of here, if I can."

"Look for one of the sergeants," she said. "Give him your statement, then you should be good to go. And don't worry about Ben. Do you know what's going on, kiddo?"

Ben shook his head. Erin ruffled his hair and smiled at him. She gave Carlyle a quick kiss on the cheek and watched them go. She felt relieved. Something awful had happened, but the people she cared about had only been on the edge of it and it hadn't had anything to do with them. Now all she had to do was her job.

She approached the blood-soaked table, trying to get a picture of what had happened. The cops who had been trying to perform first aid had given up. The man at the table was obviously dead. His throat had been opened from ear to ear.

"He's gone?" Erin asked rhetorically.

"Bled out," one of the uniforms said. "Looks like they got him in both carotids, jugular, and windpipe. Hell of a cut to make with a steak knife."

"That's the knife?" she asked, pointing to the table. A knife, identical to the ones at the other place settings, lay in a pool of blood.

"Looks like it," the cop said. "But you're the detective, so what do I know?"

Erin bent her knees to peer into the dead man's face. She saw a man who was older than he had first appeared. His eyes had crow's feet around them and his cheeks were lined and weathered. His receding hair had definitely gotten a black dye-job. She could see hints of gray around the roots. He was wearing a very expensive black pinstriped suit with a crimson necktie and matching pocket square. He also had a red carnation pinned to his coat. In short, he was the spitting image of a movie Mafia don.

"Who's this guy?" she asked, cocking a thumb at the handcuffed man.

"Martin Stracchi, according to his driver's license," another cop said, holding up the man's wallet. "Native of Manhattan. We got an address in Little Italy. Oh, and he was carrying this," he pointed to a black automatic pistol near the edge of the table, "and this," moving his finger to indicate a switchblade knife next to the gun.

"You got a permit for that gun, Mr. Stracchi?" Erin asked.

Stracchi glowered at her and shifted his shoulders, trying to get more comfortable in the handcuffs. His hands and the sleeves of his shirt were soaked with the dead man's blood.

"Doesn't matter," she added. "You'll have a record, won't you, Mr. Stracchi? And a convicted felon doesn't get a New York gun permit. Plus, that's an illegal knife. We're definitely going to have some questions to ask you."

"Detective?"

Erin turned to see a Patrol Sergeant. "What is it, Sarge?"

"This your case?"

"I guess so."

"You guess? What're you doing here, if you don't mind my asking?"

"I was trying to eat Sunday dinner. Now I'm working a homicide."

"Oh. Was wondering how a gold shield got here so fast. That's some crazy response time."

"I was here before it happened. But I didn't see much. I guess Major Crimes will play tug-of-war with the Organized Crime Task Force, and maybe the Feebies, over this one."

The Sergeant sighed. "The only thing bitter than a bureaucracy is more than one. Good luck with that, Detective. Better you than me. What do you need my guys to do?"

"Get statements from the rest of the customers," she said. "But none of them are suspects. Put out a BOLO for a guy in a white waiter's jacket and black slacks, GSW in the upper back or shoulder. He's about average height, dark hair, either white or Mediterranean complexion. And I want to talk to the manager."

The manager was a tall, graying, dignified Italian gentleman with a neat little mustache. His name was Giovanni. For a man whose restaurant had just hosted a brutal murder, he was remarkably composed. Erin met with him in his office, a dark-paneled room furnished with a heavy desk and a couple of maroon leather chairs.

"It looks like one of your waiters killed one of your customers," Erin said, not bothering with preliminaries.

"Yes, it does appear that way," Giovanni said. "It's very odd. Mr. Luna never gave any signs of abnormal behavior. This is the first time he's done anything of the sort."

Erin gave him an odd look. "I would hope so," she said. "What did you say his name was?"

"Alphonse Luna," the manager said.

"And how long has Mr. Luna been working for you?"

"Six months, give or take. I can give you the exact date of hire once I check my records. But he's been a model employee."

"What about the dead man?"

"He was not an employee," Giovanni said.

"I know that." Erin took a deep breath. "I mean, had he been in here before?"

"Oh yes. Mr. Rossi has been coming to Andolini's every Sunday for years."

That made sense. If the victim had made a habit of coming here, it would have made him vulnerable to a planned attack.

"The curious thing is," Giovanni continued, "Mr. Luna served Mr. Rossi on many occasions. They were on quite friendly terms."

"Did they have some sort of argument?" she asked.

"No, not that I heard."

"I'll need your information for Mr. Luna. Address, phone number, emergency contacts, all of it."

"Of course, Detective. Anything I can do to help."

Erin stepped out of the manager's office and fished out her phone. It was time to bring the rest of the gang on board.

Lieutenant Webb didn't answer until the fourth ring. Then, instead of his usual terse "Webb," he said, "This better be important, O'Reilly."

"Why don't you decide, sir?" she replied, nettled. After all, her day off had also been spoiled. "I was sitting down to a nice Sunday dinner at Andolini's Restaurant when one of the waiters decided to slit a customer's throat."

There was a short pause. "So, you witnessed a murder?" Webb asked.

"Yes, sir."

"And you know who did it."

"Pretty sure, sir."

"So this is open-and-shut."

"No, sir."

"Explain."

"The suspect escaped. He's injured, but he's in the wind. And I'm pretty sure he had a getaway car, which means there's probably an accomplice. Plus, our victim had a pair of bodyguards carrying illegal guns, and if they don't have records, I'll eat my own shield. Which means—"

"Organized crime hit," Webb sighed. "Yeah, I copy. Andolini's, you said?"

"Yes, sir."

"I'll be there in thirty. Call Neshenko, would you?"

"Will do."

Ready for more?

Join Steven Henry's author email list
for the latest on new releases, upcoming books and
series, behind-the-scenes details, events, and more.

Be the first to know about new releases in the Erin
O'Reilly Mysteries by signing up at
tinyurl.com/StevenHenryEmail

About the Author

Steven Henry learned how to read almost before he learned how to walk. Ever since he began reading stories, he wanted to put his own on the page. He lives a very quiet and ordinary life in Minnesota with his wife and dog.

Also by Steven Henry

Fathers
A Modern Christmas Story

When you strip away everything else, what's left is the truth

Life taught Joe Davidson not to believe in miracles. A blue-collar woodworker, Joe is trying to build a future. His father drank himself to death and his mother succumbed to cancer, leaving a broken, struggling family. He and his brother and sisters are faced with failed marriages, growing pains, and lingering trauma.

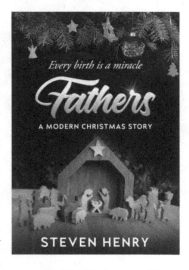

Then a chance meeting at his local diner brings Mary Elizabeth Reynolds into his life. Suddenly, Joe finds himself reaching for something more, a dream of happiness. The woodworker and the poor girl from a trailer park connect and fall in love, and for a little while, everything is right with their world.

But suddenly Joe is confronted with a situation he never imagined. What do you do if your fiancée is expecting a child you know isn't yours? Torn between betrayal and love, trying to do the right thing when nothing seems right anymore, Joe has to strip life down to its truth and learn that, in spite of the pain, love can be the greatest miracle of all.

Learn more at clickworkspress.com/fathers.

Ember of Dreams
The Clarion Chronicles, Book One

When magic awakens a long-forgotten folk, a noble lady, a young apprentice, and a solitary blacksmith band together to prevent war and seek understanding between humans and elves.

Lady Kristyn Tremayne – An otherwise unremarkable young lady's open heart and inquisitive mind reveal a hidden world of magic.

Robert Blackford – A humble harp maker's apprentice dreams of being a hero.

Master Gabriel Zane – A master blacksmith's pursuit of perfection leads him to craft an enchanted sword, drawing him out of his isolation and far from his cozy home.

Lord Luthor Carnarvon – A lonely nobleman with a dark past has won the heart of Kristyn's mother, but at what cost?

Readers love *Ember of Dreams*

"The more I got to know the characters, the more I liked them. The female lead in particular is a treat to accompany on her journey from ordinary to extraordinary."

"The author's deep understanding of his protagonists' motivations and keen eye for psychological detail make Robert and his companions a likable and memorable cast."

Learn more at tinyurl.com/emberofdreams.

More great titles from Clickworks Press

www.clickworkspress.com

The Altered Wake
Megan Morgan

Amid growing unrest, a family secret and an ancient laboratory unleash long-hidden superhuman abilities. Now newly-promoted Sentinel Cameron Kardell must chase down a rogue superhuman who holds the key to the powers' origin: the greatest threat Cotarion has seen in centuries – and Cam's best friend.

"Incredible. Starts out gripping and keeps getting better."

Learn more at clickworkspress.com/sentinel1.

Hubris Towers: The Complete First Season
Ben Y. Faroe & Bill Hoard

Comedy of manners meets comedy of errors in a new series for fans of Fawlty Towers and P. G. Wodehouse.

"So funny and endearing"

"Had me laughing so hard that I had to put it down to catch my breath"

"Astoundingly, outrageously funny!"

Learn more at clickworkspress.com/hts01.